ULTIMATELY

THE WILL OF GOD DECIDES

KATHARINA BETA

English translation from the German original title:
"Ultimately" – letztendlich gilt Gottes Wille.

Translation: Barbara Hermann

THE NEW LIGHT PUBLISHING

ULTIMATELY

THE WILL OF GOD DECIDES

KATHARINA BETA

Publisher: The New Light Publishing

Copyright 2010 all right reserved
Second edition 2012
ISBN: 9789088790294

Bibliographic Information of the German Library
The German National Library registered this
publication in the German National Library;
for detailed bibliographical data see:
http:// dnb.d-nb.de

Scripture quotations are taken from….
The New King James Bible Version (NKJV)
of the Bible Copyright 1996
by Dr. Robert H. Schuller Executive Editor
'The possibility Thinkers Bible'
Thomas Nelson Publisher, Nashville
Cover photograph taken from 'Trivial but still mysterious'
The Best from Reader's Digest, Stuttgart 1994
See 'Wonder of Nature, living relics of our past'.
Originally printed in USA
Why in the World, Reader's Digest
With kind permission of the publishers
Michael, Patricia & Susan Fogden "Wildlife Photographs".

TABLE OF CONTENTS

	Dedication of the Book
Preface:	The spirit is the wanderer
Chapter I	I have dreamed you - therefore you are
Chapter II	The dreamed one seeks the dialogue
	I take the responsibility
	Let us remain with the question
Chapter III	Valerian has no face
	Standing on the rocks
Chapter IV	Asking for the right way
Chapter V	Was I made?
Chapter VI	Thoughts about succession
	Valerian seeks the logic
Chapter VII	Include love into your deliberations
	The question of justice
Chapter VIII	The question of consciousness
	Valerian looks into the genes
	What is this, the ME
Chapter IX	What is the desire of my soul?
	A symbol
Chapter X	To be without a soul?
Chapter XI	Valerian gains wisdom
	Sources
	Indication for abbreviations and
	Terms in parentheses

DEDICATION

This book was written after my meeting with Dr. Robert H. Schuller in California, a meeting, that changed my life.
It was after Easter 2004 that I met Dr. Schuller the first time. He is one of the most inspiring personalities of the 21st century, He is a pastor with strong personal faith in the infinite power of the Lord and he manages to give others a positive way of thinking and trust in God.
I did not live without religion, but stood immobile concentrating on the head. I had read in the Bible, but I did not live in the Word. It is not important, what we think, but how we see our thoughts. The same applies to our faith and to our way of thinking. It is the distance between the head and the heart that counts.
'God does not do wonders if we ourselves do not actively participate. Even a turtle does not move on, if it does not stick it's head out of it's shell,' said Dr. Schuller.
Our faith must come out of its depths to make success possible.
Dr. Schuller spoke of his conviction that everybody can become the personality that he or she should be according to the will or plan of the Lord.
His conception that a mortal human should be willing to do the will of God, was ever present.
You have to activate your will to become the being that God intended you to be. What you need is faith and the infinite trust in God.

I have to thank Dr. Schuller for his teaching. That was the cause that made me reflect on the 'freedom of will', while I enjoyed the vast steppes of Arizona. I visited a very good friend; we had known each other for quite a long time.

My literary horizon was expanded by getting to know authors like Raymond M. Smullyan and Jorge Luis Borges. They will accompany us through this book.

Especially the philosophy of the freedom of the will be discussed.

We often think that debates lead to nothing, because so many questions remain unanswered.

When I remember the wonderful positive teaching and the optimistic influence of the words of Dr. Schuller, I have to concede that everything is possible. Free thinking strengthened my faith. My way of thinking acquired stability.

I dedicate this book to Dr. Schuller with infinite gratitude.

Katharina Beta
Author

Vienna, December 2009

*We form the vessel of moist clay
But the emptiness within
Permits to fill the jar.*

*From wood we make
Doors and windows;
But the emptiness within
Permits us to live in the house.*

*What we can see
Is deemed useful,
But the essential
Remains hidden.*

Chinese wisdom.

The spirit is the wanderer

We all know what is meant when we talk of the unbroken thread leading through an event and setting marks. So we talk of the course of life. With a small knot, or better to say a coil we start our life. Within nine months the cells are rapidly developing, enlarge, form a human body.
The end of the thread remains hidden, guarded and untouched. For a moment – in the stream of time – we thrive, we have a bit of fun and entertainment, we collect remembrances, those we would like to keep forever, then we wither and loose our form. The end of the thread will be with our children now.
The thread reaches back into the unknown to us past, it moves on into the future. Countless knobs were formed, they had their time of growth and loss, as we grow and fall into oblivion. Nothing rests but a succession of seeds.
What is changed and forms new structures as life proceeds, are not the short lived sprouts, but the inherited gifts in the thread. We all carry the spirit. How, why and where it will lead, we do not know.

On our shoulders, in our eyes, in our tortured hands we carry the entire load of what he have to bring into the future through unexplored territory, into an unknown future, a future we cannot foresee, because it is continually developing anew. We carry our burden on along with every beat of our heart, with the work of our hands and our brain we serve our creator. We stumble, hand the load over to our children, we are knocked down, fall away and are lost and forgotten. The spirit wanders on, enlarged, enriched, mysterious and multilayered.
We are used.
Should we not know who or what is using us? Who or what is it, whom we serve with such innocent loyalty?
Why are we striving without rest? What can we desire beyond what we have already gotten? What is this spirit?

Jacques Monod writes:
'From a river or a rock we know or we think that we know that they are the result of the interplay of physical forces.
With these forces we cannot correlate an image of a plan, a project or an intention. In any case not when we assume the basic premise of all processes of natural sciences, that is the premise that nature is objective and not projective.'

This basic way of thinking is highly attractive for most of us. There was a time, not so many generations back, where quite the contrary was valid.
Where rocks wanted to tumble down, rivers were rushing and roaring. Capricious spirits wandered about in the universe and used nature according to their whims. Now we know what kind of profit the understanding and power of the view brought us, where objects and processes of nature are without aim and intention. The rock has no wishes, the volcano has no aim, the river does not rush towards the sea. The wind has no destination.
There is also another perspective.
The animistic belief of the primitives is not the only alternative to scientific objectivity. This objectivity may be valid for the

periods of time in which we usually think, but this truth may expire, when time is counted in aeons.

The assumption that the light is moving in a straight line without any deviation and through adjoining mass may serve us wonderfully when we measure our land. When we want to make a picture of far away galaxies in the same way this way of thinking will lead us astray. The assumption that nature, the surrounding world is without intention will serve us well as long as we think of nature in periods of days, years and lifetimes, but will lead astray as well when eternities are at stake.

The spirit rises, substance decays. Spirit reaches out like a flame, like a speedy dance. Out of nothing it creates forms like a god, is divine. Spirit stood at the beginning, and this beginning was also the end of a former beginning and so forth.

If we go back long enough we arrive at the primordial mist, where even spirit was nothing more than atomic unrest, a throbbing being unwilling to stay motionless out in the cold. Matter desires a stable universe in a state of even distribution, immobile and inalterable.

Spirit wants to have an earth, heaven and hell, turmoil and contradiction, a brilliant sun, dispersing the darkness, shining on the good and the evil ones alike.

Matter wants thought, remembrances, desire. It wants to create a game of forms of increasing complexity and inclusivity. To strive towards a heaven that continually recedes, changing his form, then barely reaches remains just another step leading to other heavens, to the last one...

But there is no last one, since the spirit strives continually upwards, digressing, meandering, bowing, but always reaching upwards, using lower forms relentless to create higher ones, moving towards intense profoundness, consciousness, spontaneity and greater freedom.

Particles gain life. Spirit tries to tear free of substance, whereas matter tries to keep him there, to bring him to a standstill. Diminutive beings curl in the warm seas; the minute forms becoming more complex, for a moment gifted with a spiritual desire.

They meet, touch each other; spirit creates love. They touch and something is exchanged. They die and die again, without pause. Who will miss a multitude of spawn in the rivers of the past? Who would count the myriads of dancing grunions on the beaches of the primordial seas?

Who will hear the never experienced thunder of the waves of the long ago past? Who will mourn the armies of prairie rabbits, the furry masses of lemmings? They die and die and die. But they have touched each other, and something was exchanged.

Spirit arises, creates new bodies, again and again, more complex vessels to carry on the spirit, to continue to hand it on to those who will follow.

Virus changes into bacteria, they become algae, they become ferns. The force of the spirit cracks the rocks makes the tree grow.

Amoebae are in continuous movement, they extend soft stumpy arms to catch the world, to get to know it, they grow strive on, more spirit moves.

Sea flowers change into octopi, turn into fish. First they just wriggle along, then they swim then start to crawl.

Fish become snails, then lizards. Then crawl develops into walking, running and flying. Living creatures touch each other. Spirit arises among them. Shapelessness can develop fragrance, charm and fascination, even love. From the lizard to the fox, from ape to humans, in one glance, one word we find a likeness. We meet, we die, we serve the spirit without knowing it, we carry it on. The more elated the spirit, the farther it moves. We love someone far away, someone who died long ago.

***

Erich Heller writes: *'Man is the vessel of the spirit. The spirit is the traveller, who in transition through the land of the humans requests the human soul to follow him to his, the spirit's own spiritual destination.'*

Seen from nearby the path of the spirit is a wonderful way, a brilliantly glittering trace in a pitch black wood.

When you look at it from high on the small twists and turns become a straight line. Mankind has reached the ledge, from where a wide horizon opens permitting to look back into the past.

Thousands of years are clearly discernible and we can perceive the millennia hidden in the mist of antiquity.

Beyond the unsteady curves of the recent period of our way a shimmering path leads straight back into unfathomable depths.

Mankind did not start that way and will not end it. But now we move on across passes and abysses. Who made this way we are going? It was not man. Our footprints just started alongside it. Life did not start here. Because the way reaches past even beyond the beginning of life.

Spirit is the wanderer. It is he who traverses the realm of mankind. We did not make the spirit, it is not our possession, we can not enclose it, we are only carrying it on. We take it over from never mourned and forgotten forms, carry it through the time given to us and will hand it on enriched or diminished, to those who come after us.

Spirit is the wanderer we are the means of transport.

Spirit creates and spirit destroys. Creation without destruction is impossible. Destruction without creation feeds on bygone creation, reduces form to matter and strives towards immobility.

Spirit creates more than it destroys, though not in every season, not even in every age; this causes the turns, these turns to the past, where the matter's desire for immobility triumphs in destruction, but the force of creation leads to this endless striving straight way forwards.

From the primary mist of the matter to the spiral nebula of the milky ways, to the order of solar systems, from melted rock to an earth of air, land and water, from the abyss to the light, to life, from feeling to recognition, from memory to awareness, man has become the mirror, where the spirit is reflected. In the river currents turn back, vortexes are swirling.

The river itself stops, recedes, reappears, flows on. The development of form, growing awareness, of moving from matter to consciousness, towards thinking, this is the main direction. The harmony of mankind with nature consists in the continuation of this journey on its ancient track, towards a greater freedom and a deeper awareness. *'We are machines programmed to survive,'* stated Richard Dawkins[1]. *'We are blindly programmed to sustain the egoistic molecules, called Genes. This is a truth that still evokes amazement. Though this has been know for years, we simply cannot adapt to it. What remains is the hope that we can contrive to bring others towards this astonishment.'*

The beginning was elementary. It is difficult to explain how a simple universe came into being. Even more difficult to explain the sudden appearance of a completely developed complex order, of life, or the being that was capable of creating life.

---

[1] Extract from Richard Dawkins: 'On not knowing how to live' by Allen Wheelis.

CHAPTER I

I have dreamed you - therefore you are

Nobody saw the canoe sink into the mud. Nobody saw him going to shore in the depth of the night. Several days had passed before the inhabitants of the little village detected that a taciturn man from the south had come.
His home was one of the numerous villages at the upper course of the river. A small place situated on a steep mountain slope, where the language had no distinct sound.
They all talked about how the silent man had kissed the mud of the river bank. He had hurt his hands when he pulled himself up to the river bank.

Bleeding he staggered towards the wall of the temple. A wall adorned with images of horses and tigers, cut into the stone. The outskirts of the temple showed the traces of old burns. Shrubs thrived in the swamp surrounding it. High trees grew between them, though you could not call it a wood. Maybe a long time ago there had been one, when tigers and horses wore the colours of fire. Now they were grey as ash.
The silent stranger lay down and rested besides the large sculptures.
As the warmth of the sun gained strength he awoke.
Calmly he registered that his wounds had healed.
He closed his eyes and went back to sleep, as if he had been ordered to do so, as if it was his duty to fall asleep.
The man knew that this temple was the place of his destination. He saw that the abundantly growing trees and shrubs had not yet succeeded to overgrow the ancient walls. About midnight the cry of a bird awakened him.
Traces of unshod feet, some figs and a jug of water told him that the villagers had watched him in his sleep.
They were afraid of ancient magic. Fear shook him. In the decaying wall he searched for a n aperture, maybe an old tomb and there he hid under unknown foliage.

He was driven by a deep instinct, not something simple but a metaphysical force.
He wanted to dream and in dreaming to create a human.
He wanted to dream him into reality with every detail and force reality to accept him.
This magic purpose devoured his entire soul. If someone had asked him his name, he would not have known the answer. If someone had inquired into his former life there would have been nothing but silence. The uninhabited ruins of the temple gave him an opportunity. They admitted only a minimum of the visible world. The villagers around were no real problem. They brought him simple food, rice and fruit. It was enough for him. He had only one purpose: to sleep and to dream.
In the beginning his dreams were chaos. But with time they took on a dialectic form The stranger dreamed himself into the centre stage of a circular amphitheatre.
Lots of silent disciples sat on the steps. Their faces seemed to be aeons away although clearly discernible. A man held lectures on anatomy, cosmography and about the soul. The faces listened intently.
They were trying hard to give prudent answers, as if they knew the final aim of this test, that one of them could be released from this empty spurious state and be admitted into the real world.
In his dreams and when awake the man considered the answers his ghosts had given. Fraud could not impress him and in some questions he found a growing understanding. He was searching for a soul worthy to participate in the workings of the universe. When ten nights had passed he recognized with bitterness, that nothing could be expected from the passive ones of the disciples, whereas something could be expected made from those who voiced reasonable disagreement.
The first, though they earned love and compassion, would never become individuals, the others were more promising.
Soon he dreamed as well in the afternoons, only in the morning he was awake for a short time.
One afternoon he relinquished the imaginary college forever only one disciple could remain with him.

He was a thin, reserved young man, sometimes unruly, whose sharp features resembled the man who had dreamed him.

Some time he was quite cast down because of the sudden loss of his fellow students. The progress he made in the private lessons amazed his teacher. Then disaster struck.

He awoke from sleep as if coming out of a sticky slimy plain. He saw the light of the fading day and at first he mistook it for the glimmer of dawn. Then he knew that there had been no dreams.

During this night and into the following morning restless sleeplessness took him. He decided to walk into the woods and vent his strength in movement. All he got was a thread of a thin slumber slightly embellished with raw chaotic useless viewings. He tried to revive the college again.

Just when he had spoken the magical words it formed only vaguely and disappeared. Tears burned in his old eyes all the endless hours he had to stay awake.

At last he understood that the task of forming the ever moving substance of dreams and hold it at some point was quite exacting.

He had tried to enter into the mysteries of the higher and lower orders, but it was more enacting for him that to weave a rope out of sand or stamp a coin out of volatile wind.

He understood further that this breakdown at the beginning was inevitable. He swore to erase the gigantic hallucination that had lead him astray from his mind. At the same time he searched for another method to go to work. But before he began again he took his time to restore his strength that the feverish illusions had cost him.

He stopped to dream on purpose and finally achieved that he could spend the better part of the day asleep.

In the first moments he dreamed of a beating heart. In his dream the heart was moving, warm of life and secret.

It had the size of a balled fist and hang, a purple oval, in the mists of a human body. The body had neither face nor sex.

With intense love he dreamed of it during the following two weeks of moonlit nights.

In each consecutive night the heart become more vivid.

He did not touch it. He was content to see it and to watch it and to follow it with his gaze. He was aware of it and felt it from various distances and at different angles. In the fourteenth night he stroked along the main artery with his index finger and then stroked the entire heart, the inside and the outside. He was content with the inspection. In wise deliberation he spent one night without dreaming. Then he touched the heart anew, called the name of a planet and started to view another vital organ.

Before a year had passed he had made the skeleton and the eyelids.

He encountered great difficulties with the innumerable quantity of hair on the head. He dreamed a fully grown man, a young man. But the young man could not sit up, he could not talk and he would not open his eyes.

The dreaming wizard dreamed him night for night. In the ancient Gnostic cosmic mysteries the magicians moulded a raw Adam, who could not stand upright. As clumsy and raw and elemental as this peace of clay Adam was the dreamed Adam the magician had wrought in these nights.

Once the desperate wizard was near to destroy his handiwork, but he could not. In vain he prayed to all the spirits of earth and water, he fell to his knees at the feet of the statue of the deity and prayed for unknown help.

At sunset he began to dream about a statue. He dreamed it coming to life, filling it with life. It was no ungainly crossover between a tiger and a horse, but it was both creatures at the same time, but also a bull, a rose, a storm.

This multiform being told him that its name on earth was fire, that in this circular temple sacrifices had been given to him and that by his magic he would give life to the dreamed man of mist, that all creatures, with the exception of the fire itself and the dreamer should see a real human made of flesh and bone in him.

He ordered that the one after being instructed in the ancient rites, should be sent to the other now ruined temple, whose pyramids at the downside course of the river were still habitable, so that a voice should proclaim again his mane in the relinquished shrine.

While the magician dreamed on, in this dream the dreamed man woke to life and he followed the instructions he had received.

At first, within a period that lasted two years, he dedicated himself to instruct his creature in the secrets of the cosmic forces and the worship of fire. It pained him to the core of his heart that he should let his handiwork go.

Under the pretext of vital scholarly necessities he expanded the hours dedicated to slumber more and more every day. Under close scrutiny he found that he had not made the right shoulder correctly and redid it. Then he suffered from the impression that all this had already happened before...

Altogether these days were filled with happiness. When he closed his eyes he thought:

'Now I will be with my creature.' Or, but more seldom: 'The son I made is waiting for me and he will not be there if I do not go to him.'

Step by step he accustomed him to reality. Once he ordered him to set up a flag on the top of a far away hill.

On the next day the banner was flying from the hilltop.

He taught him other, similar accomplishments, requiring more and more audacity. Not without bitterness he found that his son was ready to be born, maybe even waiting for this.

That night he kissed him the first time and told him to go to the other temple, whose ruins were situated down river, the path leading through impenetrable forests and swamps. Now the magician erased all remembrances of the disciple's student years, so that the son should never find out, that he was of his making. He should consider himself a man, like all the others.

His victory and his peace were marred by satiety.

In the dawn of morning and the shadows of the evening he grovelled before the stone statue. In his head he pondered the thoughts that his unreal son would carry out the same rites in the ruins of the other temple, far down the river.

In the nights his dreams did not show the youngster, he had ordinary dreams like other humans.

The sounds and colours of the world remained hazy for him. The absent son still drew the live force out of his soul. The laws of life had been fulfilled. The wise one remained in a state of trance.

After a long time, some people said it must have been years, others believed it had been decades, he awoke at midnight, by the noise caused by two men rowing a boat.

He could not recognize their faces.

The men told him the story of a mighty magician in the temple of the north, whose strength was such that he could walk through fire and never burned.

The wizard remembered the words of the divinity and he was convinced that of all creatures living on earth only the fire would know that his son was a spirit.

This insight gave him peace, but it did not last and started to torture him. He began to fear that his son would start to make inquiries about this extraordinary gift and would then find out about his odd nature.

To find out that he was no human being, but just the emanation of somebody else's dream and feel unfathomable humiliation and shame. Every father is concerned about the fate of his sons, the sons he begot in sensuous rapture and felicity.

How understandable that the magician feared for the future of this son whom he had made part by part in one thousand and one secret nights of dreams. His doubts and fears found a sudden end. The first signs of the foretold end appeared. After a long draught he could make out a small cloud behind the far away hills, small like a little bird. The sky in the south turned pink, then a sooty red, mists sprang up and shrouded the metal of the ruins in rust. The animals fled in haste.

What had happened centuries ago happened again.

The ruins of the temple dedicated to the god of fire burned in bright flames.

On the morning when all birds had gone, the magician saw the ring of fire tightening around the walls.

One moment he wanted to flee into the fire until he understood that death was approaching to crown his age and relieve him from his sufferings[2].

We advanced towards the ring of fire, the flames did not bite into his flesh, they caressed him and rushed into him without heat or burn. Relieved, ashamed and appalled he realized that he as well was only an image, someone else had dreamed him.

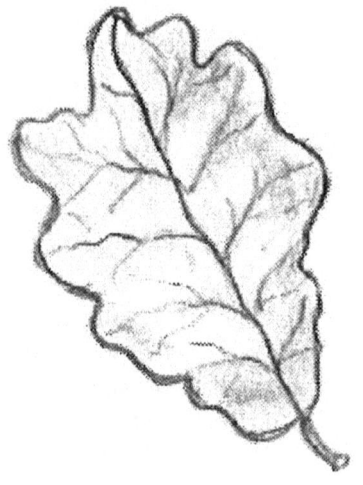

---

[2] Extracts from: Jorge Borges 'Labyrinthe'

*Thus you order and hand out
Reason, law and life,
Carried by waves of fire
they fill the world.
The Lord of the Heavens,
The Ruler of the Universe
Gives life to the gigantic and glittering
stars in heaven, to the howling winds,
to creatures and flowers,
to all things that breathe*

CHAPTER II

The dreamed one seeks the dialogue

The son made, called by his name Valerian, tried to find a part of the divine wisdom by touching fire and water.
He sat at the enclosure of the large ancient well and observed the snake devouring the herb that gives the force of life, a herb that grew at the banks of the river.
He jumped and tried to catch the reptile to take its bounty, but the snake escaped. He followed it crawling along. Just as he extended his hands to catch it something strange happened. The snake got off again, it shook off the old skin and glided away, beautiful and rejuvenated.
The old skin remained behind. Valerian took up the empty skin. He screamed once in pain and then he lay on the ground motionless.
As the excitement slowly ebbed away he heard a voice in his heart:
"Valerian, you will not find the life that you seek."
He looked into the direction where the snake had disappeared and thought:
'What sort of life do I seek? Do I seek? He got an answer:
"You are seeking the real life, the unchangeable and lasting

life. *But beware: you will have to try many paths and you will endure many changes."*

Valerian recognized suddenly that he was more than the snake that he differed vastly from the creature. What he had seen happen to the snake made him understand that there must be something else than the outer hull, that this example was meant for him, for his inner life, his core.

He realized that on the way he had gone through in his dream, and when he had awakened from his sleep, he had become his own self. The image occurred that likewise he would pass on into death, changed but still himself in a new form of existence. In this way moves the universe, in this way things appear for ever and silently in space and time.

***

Valerian lived within time. The thread was still coiled up.
Slowly it began to unfold as Valerian started his wandering.
When he arrived in the ruins of the holy temple he called: "God, I am a living being, I want to be connected to you, if I have to live here and then I will have a greater freedom. I am sure that I will encounter many human problems. You have the freedom to get to their roots."
God:
"You should listen to the voices that you heard never before. Open up to the possibility that there is a living God, who loves you. Maybe he has been looking for you already a long time in order to help you. There are a lot of worlds within this world and the best and most intelligent living creatures never yet had any contact with these other realities of my universe. I know who you are, wherever you are, whatever you do, awake or dreaming. I am telling you what reality is. I do exist."

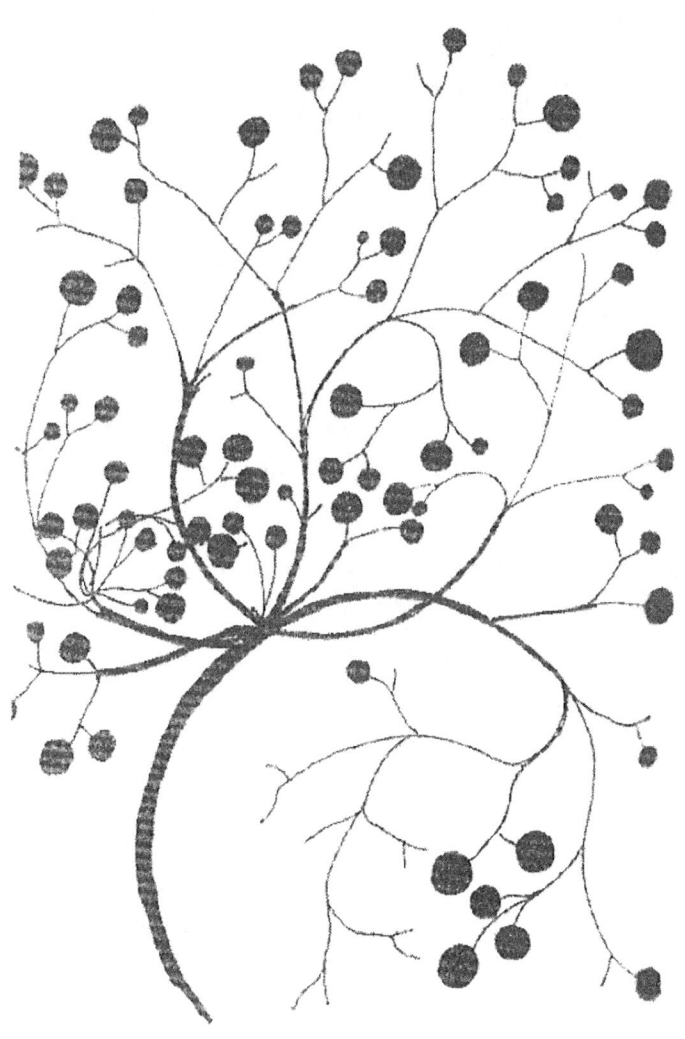

Valerian:
"You are the eternal spiritual universal being, that we call God?"

God:
"Yes. Since you came into being I often tried to contact your mind, your positive thought, feelings, impulses, reminiscences and presumptions that are continuously entering your consciousness. Something that helps to give you a positive feeling of life could already be a message, a hint of my presence."

Valerian:
The bible pretends to be your voice and your word for all humans on this earth. In this book we read words that someone called Matthew wrote down (28:20). 'And this you should know: I am always with you every day until the end of the world."

God:
"I can inspire you, or send you thoughts and feelings. With six billion human beings living on this earth I have all the possibilities of a large communication network. As long as people can see, hear or have perception, as long as another human being can influence you in any way, it may happen that I am sending you a message this way. I know you all and I am concerned about all of you."

Valerian:
"You have contact with all of them, even when they do not believe in you, or cannot be bothered with you?"

God:
"Yes. Open up to the feeling, that I can be seen and heard in everything and in everyone. Thus you will learn to regard any grief that will surely happen to you, less than a single event, but more as a sort of process. Suffering is not something you can put off. It is enduring. Its contours change in the course of time. Therefore it is important for you to learn and understand that your reaction has the power, more than anything else in the world, to form the kind of pain. That is the cause why positive attitudes are so important. Try to think: you can diminish the negative consequences of pain within your life.

You can change your life in such a way that even a fiend might become a helpful friend."

Valerian:

"Changes happen. The world around me is changing. My course of life is changing. Also the perspective, where I made my first painful experiences, will change. My needs will change. My wishes will change. Is it assured that the perception of my pain is also an ongoing process?"

God:

"Believe in it. Do not forget, I did promise: if your faith in me is only as large as a mustard seed, you can move a mountain. Nothing will be impossible for you."

Valerian:

"What would be the worst that could happen to me?"

God:

"The worst will be that what you think of as the worst for yourself. You will find out when you encounter it.
Thousands of beings have met the worst on their way of life. They were not overwhelmed by it, often they vanquished it.
In case you meet your worst fate, then you will feel the spiritual power existing in you. I never send anyone more than he can bear."

Valerian:

"I presume that riddles and secrets are difficult for me to endure, they create fear and kindled by negative illusions comes the question again: what is the worst that could happen to me?"

God:

"Well I do know this. My counsel is: take up the feeling that you are a human being inspired by me and you will be strong enough to counter the worst. Complacent you will look death in the face some day. Please start to see all possibilities in a positive light."

Valerian:

"How am I to do this?"

God:

"Look upon your path and on what you have and what you are. Do not look at that what you lost. Ask yourself:

What did remain for me? Your friends? Your freedom?
The freedom to enter new relationships, to make new decisions?
Arrange your values anew? Listen to my voice in your heart, that will tell you: 'Come on it is time to go on your way.' Look out for the possibilities to do good deeds."
Valerian:
"Why?"
God:
"That is the word that all creatures are crying out into the darkness in their pain."
Valerian:
"Why?"
God:
"I cannot answer this question. On principle I avoid giving answers to questions starting with the word 'why'."
Valerian:
"When I ask you during my grief and my pain for the why, I do not think that I expect an answer. I just want to set a distance between me and the darkness around me. If you gave me an answer, more questions would arise. I could provoke you to answer me. But why just me?"
God:
"Why? It is a normal, understandable and justified question. I did not say that it was not justifiably asked. But understand that there is no necessity to answer it. For as long as these questions remain without an answer, you are forced to trust me infinitely in times of impenetrable darkness. If I would give convenient answers to my creatures when they are suffering, they could understand the purpose of suffering and they would start to get dependent on being able to understand. They would become addicted to find the cause. That is a way to undermine faith."
Valerian:
"You want to tell me that I have to find my spiritual maturity in order to counter unfathomable vexations with a positive attitude? My God, I do not understand it but I will try to trust you."

God:
"Your faith will grow when you learn to trust in me, when you do not see a sense and get no answer."
Valerian:
"Then true reality is a secret?"
God:
"You are speaking of a secret when things seem inexplicable to you."
Valerian:
"I mean those questions, where I do not get an answer."
God:
"A secret occurs when you are confronted with challenges that are contrary to all your experiences."
Valerian:
"I am speaking of a secret, when I have to admit that I do not know an answer, or found only answers that are not satisfactory."
God:
"Secrets are my gift for humans. The strategy is to incite personalities to find their greatest possible development."
Valerian:
"Do you mean the forming of the character? Is this the process?"
God:
"Yes, but also the possibility to become a better, more mature personality."
Valerian:
"I do not know how that would help in a torrent of confusion, if I could cope with this, even if I tried very hard."
God:
"Beware of men who presume to know it all."
Valerian answered slowly and intonated softly each word: "I have been told that you are a merciful God. Therefore I place a humble request before you and implore you to
fulfil it. Liberate me from the compulsion to have a free will."
God:
"You dare to reject my great gift?"

Valerian:
"How can you call a gift, what has been forced on me. I do have a will, but not by my own decision. I never freely decided to have a free will. I am forced to have a free will, if I want it or not."

God:
"Why would you prefer to have no free will?"

Valerian:
"Freedom of will means personal ethical responsibility. That is a rather heavy burden."

God:
"You feel that ethical responsibility is a burden?"

Valerian:
"Frankly speaking I can not explain why it is so, I only know that it is."

God:
"Well, if that is so let us presume that I will free you of all moral responsibility, but I would leave you your free will. Would you then be content?"

Valerian after a short break:
"No, I am afraid, I would not be content."

God:
"I thought so. Moral responsibility is not the only point that makes you dislike freedom of will. What else about free will disturbs you?"

Valerian:
"Freedom of will gives me the capability for sin. But I do not want to commit sin."

God:
"If you do not want to sin, why would you commit it?"

Valerian:
"Dear Lord, How should I know why I commit a sin. I do it. Vile temptations do influence me. I cannot withstand them, even if I do try."

God:
"If it is really true that you can not withstand them, then you do not sin out of your free will, therefore you will not commit a sin in my understanding."

Valerian:
"No, I do have the feeling that I could remain without a sin if only I would try harder. By my knowledge the will is infinite. If one does not want to sin with all one's heart, then one will not commit sin."

God:
"Well you really should know how hard you try not to commit a sin."

Valerian:
"But honestly, I do not know. When it happens I have the feeling that I do all that my own strength permits, but when I look back, doubt will arise that I did not do everything possible."

God:
"In other words, you do not even know if you did sin. So there is the other possibility that you did not commit a sin at all."

Valerian:
"Of course there is this possibility, but also the other one that I did fall into sin. This is what scares me."

God:
"Why are you afraid of the thought that you could have fallen into sin?"

Valerian quite desperate:
"I do not know why. One of the causes may be that you are said to punish people in the life after death."

God:
"If this causes you distress, why did you not say so from the start. You make a long speech about freedom of will and responsibility and never touch the core of the matter. Why did you not just ask me not to punish you for your sins?"

Valerian:
"I am probably realistic enough to understand that you would not grant such a request."

God:
"You do not mean it. You presume to have a realistic impression to know which petitions I do grant? Listen what I will do. I will give you a special licence to commit as many sins as you want to.

And I give you my divine word of honour that you will not be punished in the slightest for them. Do you agree?"
Valerian looked up deeply distressed.
"Please, do not do that."
God:
"Why not? Do you not trust my word, the word of your Lord?"
Valerian:
"Of course I do trust. But please understand, I do not want to sin. I deeply loathe sin even without the threat of possible punishment for me later."
God:
"If that is so, then I do have something even better for you. I could take away your loathing for sin. Now you swallow this miraculous pill and you will loose all your loathing of sin. You will commit sin with lust and love, you will not feel remorse nor loathing. Furthermore I will grant you freedom of punishment for your sins. You will feel wonderful in all eternity. Here try the pill."
Valerian:
"No, I will not."
God:
"Is that not quite unreasonable? I will even take away your loathing of sin, the last hindrance to commit one."
Valerian remains stubborn.
"No I will not take the pill."
God:
"Why do you refuse?"
Valerian:
"I do believe you that the pill will take away my loathing of sin, but the repugnance I feel now is too great and it will deter me to take it."
God:
"I can order you to swallow the pill."
Valerian:
"I do not want to take it."
God:
"You do not want to take it out of your own free will?"

Valerian:
"Yes."
God:
"Well it seems that you can use your freedom of will quite properly."
Valerian now doubtful:
"I do not understand…"
God:
"Are you not content now that you have a free will, so that you could reject my dangerous offer? How would you find it, if I forced you to take the pill, if you wanted it or not."
Valerian:
"Please do not do that."
God:
"Of course not. I just wanted to explain something to you. Let us try in another way. Instead of forcing you to swallow the pill I will grant your original prayer to take away your free will. But the promise holds that you will take the pill in the moment your freedom of will is gone."
Valerian:
"How should I decide to take the pill if I do not have a will any more ?"
God:
"I did not say that you will decide to take it. I told you the rules, as the saying goes, these rules will ensure that you take the pill."
Valerian:
"I will still refuse."
God:
"You reject my offer to take away your freedom of will. This is vastly different from your first petition and prayer I think."
Valerian is quite relieved.
"Now I can see what your intentions were. Your line of argument is ingenuous, but I am not sure if it is true. There are some points to be discussed."
God:
"I do not doubt it."

Valerian:
"You spoke of two things and they are contrary to my sentiments. First you told me that one can sin only out of one's own free will. Then you wanted to give me a pill that could take away my freedom of will. Then I could sin as much as I wanted. Now I ask you, how could I, if we follow your first statement, be at all capable to commit a sin?"
God:
"You confuse two different parts of our discussion. I never told you that the pill would take away your freedom of will, it would only take away your loathing of sin."
Valerian:
"I feel quite confused."
God:
"Let us start again. Let us presume that I agree to take away your freedom of will, so that you can them commit countless actions that you now consider sinful. Strictly spoken you will not commit then any sins, because your actions will not be based on your free will.
Then these actions will be free from all ethical responsibility and no punishment for sin could
follow. But all these actions will be of a kind that you now deem sinful. They will have all the attributes that you loathe now, only your loathing will have ceased.
Then you will feel no abhorrence for these deeds."
Valerian:
"I abhor such actions now and that is enough to reject your offer."
God:
"Well, I ask you again and I repeat: Do I understand that you no longer want me to take away your freedom of will?"
Valerian hesitates.
"I think it is so."
God:
"Agreed: Could you tell me why now you do not want to be unburdened from your freedom of will? Can you tell me why?"

Valerian:
"Because, as you explained to me, without a free will I would commit a lot more sins than now."
God patiently: *"Did I not explain to you that without a freedom of will you cannot sin at all."*
Valerian:
"If I now decide to be liberated from my freedom of will, than all my misdeeds in the future will not be a sin, but all of them together will be the sin of this moment, when I decided to abandon my free will."
God:
"That sounds as if you were in dire straits."
Valerian:
"Of course I do have difficulties. You led me into this dilemma. Whatever I do, it will be wrong. If I keep my freedom of will I will continue to fall into sin. If I abandon my freedom of will with your assistance, then I will commit a sin now because I agree."
God:
"This will not lead you into difficulties. I am quite prepared to leave you your freedom of will or to take it away, according to your wish. But neither one or the other will make you feel content. I would like to help you, but seemingly I can not."
Valerian:
"Very true."
God:
"This is not my fault. Why are you so enraged?"
Valerian:
"Because you brought me into that embarrassing situation."
God:
"According to your own statements there is nothing I could have done to satisfy you."
Valerian:
"You mean that now there is nothing that could satisfy me. That does not mean that there is nothing that you could have done before all this."
God:
"What should I have done in the past?"

Valerian:
"Evidently you should never have granted me a free will. Now that you have given it to me, it is too late. Now whatever I do, it will be wrong. You should never have given me a free will."
God:
"I understand. Why are you of the opinion that it would have been preferable that I never granted you a free will?"
Valerian:
"Because then I would have been incapable to commit a sin.
God:
"I like to learn from former mistakes."
Valerian:
"What do you mean?"
God:
"Oh I know this might be a logical paradox. You were instructed to believe that every thinking being commits a moral sin if he is convinced that I could make a mistake. On the other hand there is nothing that I would not have the right to do. But I am also a being with feelings. The question now is, do I have the right or do I not have the right to state that I might commit an error."
Valerian:
"Are you kidding? One of your statements is wrong. I was not instructed that every feeling being commits an offence in doubting your omniscience. Only that this was an offence done by mortals. Since you are immortal this does not apply to you."
God:
"You are seeing this from a rational point of view. I suspected you suffered a shock when I told you that I always learned from my mistakes."
Valerian:
"Of course I was shocked. Not because of the logical paradox as you called it in jest.
Not because I felt that you had no right to give such a statement, but purely because of the circumstance that you uttered such words at all.
I have been firmly instructed that you never make mistakes.

Therefore I was quite taken aback abut your statement that you could make mistakes."

God:

"I never stated that this is possible. I only said that if I made mistakes it would be a pleasure to learn from them. This does not imply that it could be the case."

Valerian:

"Please let us cease splitting hairs on this issue. Did you or did you not admit that it was a mistake to grant me freedom of will?"

God:

"Well, I just wanted to propose to make a distinction here. Let us recapitulate your present distress. You do not want to have a free will, because with a free will you can commit sin. You do not want to fall into sin, although I find this quite entertaining. Somehow you want to fall into sin otherwise you would not do it. But let us leave that behind. If on the other hand you declare that you want to give away your freedom of will then you would now take up the responsibility for all your future actions. Thus I should not have given you a freedom of will at all."

Valerian:

"Quite right." He breathed deeply as if freed from an enormous burden.

God:

"I can understand your concern. Many mortals, among them some theologians, did complain that I gave them their freedom of will without asking them beforehand, and then make them solely responsible for their actions. In other words they have the feeling that they have to fulfil a contract with me, a contract they never consented to."

Valerian felt better and agreed:

"Quite right."

God:

"I can understand their feelings. Maybe their complaints are justified. But the complaints are based on an unrealistic understanding of the relevant facts. About these circumstances I would like to enlighten you.

I think these revelations will come as a surprise to you. Instead of giving you a tedious lesson I will apply the process of Socrates. Let us recall. You regret that I gave you a free will. I maintain that when you understand the true problem of the matter your regret will cease to exist.

I stating the case I tell you now what I want to do. I intend to create a new universe, a new continuity in time and space. Into this new universe a mortal being will be born, your likeness to the last hair, we could say, you will be reborn. To this new mortal, another you, I could give freedom of will or not. What would you prefer?"

Valerian, feeling highly relieved: "Please, spare him to have a free will.

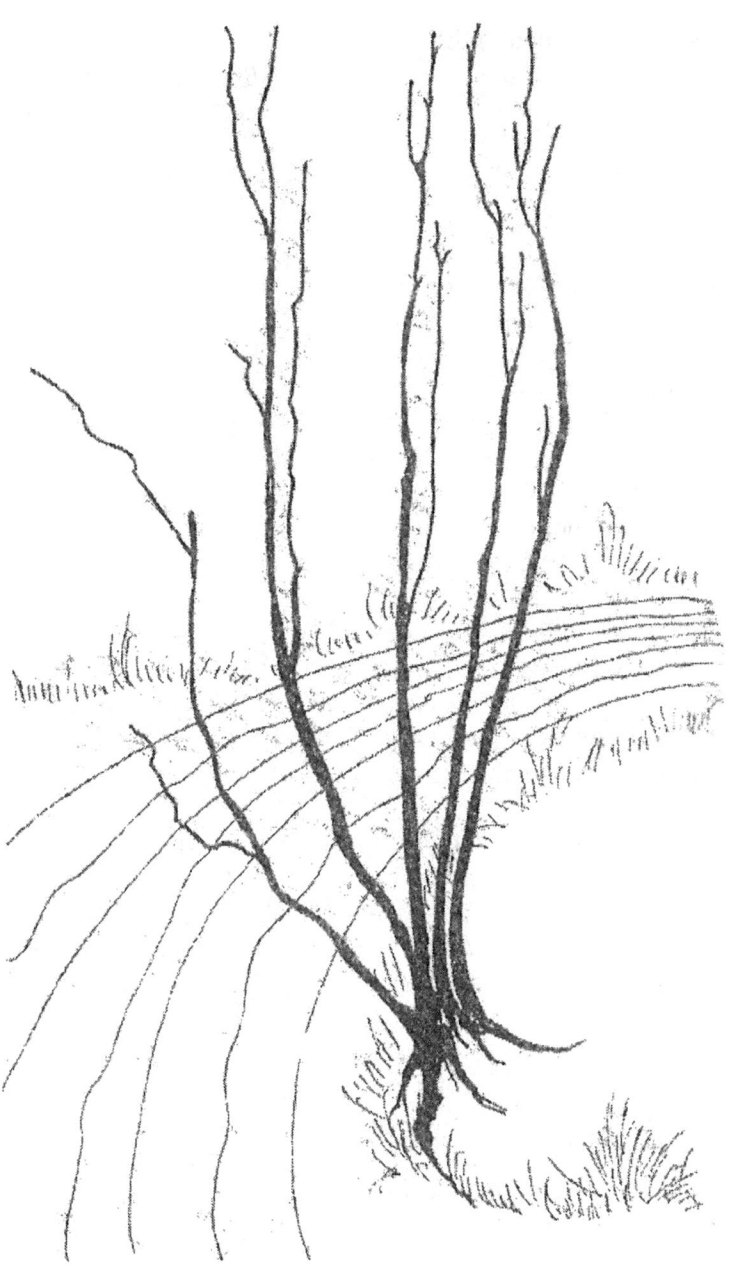

I take the responsibility

God, patiently and with indulgence:
»*All right. I will accept your advice. But you do realise, that then this new You will commit the vilest atrocities of all kinds.*«
Valerian:
»But they will not be sins, since he will not have freedom of will.«
God:
»*Call it sin or whatever. The fact remains that these will be terrible deeds, in the sense that they will cause a lot of pain for other feeling creatures.*«
Valerian, after a short pause:
»Dear Lord, I am in trouble again. Always the same. If I give you the green light now to create this new being without any freedom of will, who will commit nevertheless vile atrocities, then he will not commit sins, of course, but I, who permitted this, will be the sinner myself.«
God:
»*In this case, I suggest something preferable. Listen. I have already decided, if I will make this new*
You with or without freedom of will. Now I will write my decision on this scrap of paper. Later on I will show it to you. But my decision has been made now. My decision is irrevocable.
You will never have the opportunity to change it. You will bear no responsibility in this case.
What I would like to know from you now is, what do you hope, that my decision will be? But consider, the responsibility is only mine. It does not concern you in any way. Therefore you can tell me openly and without fear what do you hope my decision will be?«
Valerian, after a very long pause:
»I do hope you decided to grant him a free will.«
God:
»*How very interesting. So I removed the last obstacle from your path.*

If I would deny him a free will, then nobody could commit sin again. So why do you hope, that I will grant him freedom of will?«
Valerian:
»Because sin or no sin, the decisive point is, that a being without a free will would move about - according to what you said earlier - and hurt other beings, and I would not want this.«
God, sighing in infinite relief:
»Finally, finally you comprehend, what this is all about.«
Valerian, slightly hesitating:
»What this is about?«
God:
»Well the real problem is not that sin is committed.
The important thing is, that no harm should be done, no pain caused to human beings and other feeling creatures.«
Valerian:
»You sound like an utilitarian.«
God: *»Well, I am utilitarian.«* [3]
Valerian:
»What ?«
God:
»Whatever, however, whoever - fact is, I am an utilitarian. No Unitarian mind, but utilitarian.«
Valerian:
»I can't believe it.«
God:
»I know. In your religious instruction you were taught differently. Your ideas covet the Kantian way of thinking, not the utilitarian one. You were simply not properly instructed.«
Valerian seems unsettled.
He does not dare to take a breath, at last he stammers: »I do not know what to say.«

---

[3] Utilitarianism is not widely known, this is a philosophical and ethical doctrine, equaling the ethical with the useful (utilitarian, thus the usefulness for the single person or for the entire society is the ultimate goal or purpose.

God:
»Well, you do not know what to say. That may be a good point, you clearly have a tendency of talking too much. Now seriously, why do you think, did I bless you with a free will?«
Valerian seems astonished:
»Yes, why? I never thought much about the why. I was only of the opinion, that you should not have done it. But why you did do it? The only thing I recall on that is the well known theological explanation: without a free will nobody could acquire salvation or damnation. Without a free will one cannot acquire the right for a life in eternity.«
God:
»How very interesting. I do have eternal life. Do you presume, hat I had to earn it?«
Valerian quickly:
»Of course not. With you this is different. I was taught that you are perfection itself. Therefore you do not have to earn eternal life.«
God:
»Really? Well my position thus is enviable.«
Valerian:
»Well I do not understand, what you mean.«
God:
»I enjoy eternal bliss and I never had to suffer for it or bring a sacrifice. I never had to resist temptation or some such thing. Without any such merit I rejoice in eternal, blessed life. You poor mortals have to endure and torment yourselves, go through all sorts of moral conflicts. And what for? You do not even know, if I really exist or not. Do you know if there is a life after death? And if so, how would that concern me? How much you strive and try to get my mercy by being 'good', you can never be sure, that the best you have to give, is really good enough for me. Therefore you can never be sure, that salvation will be granted to you. Just think, mine is already what equals your salvation, but I never had to go through this long and painful process to deserve it. Do you envy me now?«
Valerian:
»To envy You, would be blasphemy.«

God:
»*Come on now. Don't be a bore. You do not talk to your teacher of catechism, you are talking to ME. The matter is not if you have, or have not the right to be envious, but if you do envy me. Well, do you?*«

Valerian in truthful frankness:
»Well of course, I do.«

God:
»*Indeed, as you see the world now, you can only be envious, but with a more realistic view of the world; I think you will cease to be so. You really adopted this conception you have been taught, that your life on earth is a sort of testing period, and you have been given the free will, so that you can prove your worthiness for a blessed, eternal life. But what astonishes me is, if you really believe, that I am as merciful as my worshippers praise me, then why should I demand that humans have to earn such things as happiness and eternal life. Why would I not grant these things to all creatures, regardless if they deserve it or not?*«

Valerian:
»I was instructed, that your moral law, your sense of justice, requires that good thoughts and deeds will be rewarded with happiness, and bad thoughts and deeds punished by pain and suffering.«

God:
»*Then you were not instructed correctly.*«

Valerian:
»But religious literature is filled with these teachings. Take for example Jonathan Edward's 'Sinners in the hand of an irate God'. He writes, how you hold your enemies, like repellent scorpions, above the flames of the hellish dragon, only some remnants of mercy keeping you from letting them fall into the pit to earn the fate that they deserve.«

God:
»*I am glad, that I never had to endure the tirades of this Mister Jonas Edwards. Seems to me, that is one of the worst misleading sermons ever held. Beware, alone the title 'Sinners*

in the hand of an irate God' speaks for itself. First of all: I am never irate.
Second: I do not think in notions like sin or no sin. Third: I do not have enemies.«
Valerian sceptical:
»Do you want to say that there is no one you hate; or that there is nobody who hates you?«
God:
The first statement is right, for the latter there might be some that hate me.«
Valerian:
»I beg your pardon, but I do know people who declared in public that they did hate you. Sometimes I also hate you.«
God:
»Then you hate the image you yourself made of me. That is not the same as hating me as I really am.«
Valerian:
»Do you want to say, that it is not wrong to hate a false image of you, but it would be improper to hate you as you really are?«
God:
»No, that is not what I wanted to say. What I had in mind is something more profound. My words have nothing to do with doing right or wrong. What I wanted to express is, that someone who would know me as I am, would not have the mental capacity to hate me.«
Valerian astonished, is stammering:
»Could you explain, why, when we mortals have such a false conception of your true nature, you do not show us the truth? Why do you not lead us on to the right path?«
God:
»What makes you think that I do not do that?«
Valerian:
»I am thinking, why then do you not appear before us in a visible form and tell us how wrong we are.«
God:
»Are you such a simpleton to believe that I am one of the beings, that can be perceived by your senses? It would be more

appropriate to say that I am your senses.«
Valerian, this time quite astonished, asks:
»You are my senses?«
God:
»That is quite inaccurate. I am more that that. But it is nearer to the truth than the notion, that you could be aware of me by help of your senses. I am not an object. As you are a being, so am I. A being has awareness, but cannot be perceived.
You cannot see me as you can see your own thoughts. You can see an apple, but the process of being aware of the apple, cannot be seen. And I am much nearer to the process of seeing the apple that the apple itself. You can see the pips of the apple.
I see the apples in the pips.«
Valerian:
»If I cannot see you, how do I know then if you exist?«
God:
»A good question. But how did you get to know if I exist?«
Valerian:
»Well, I am talking to you, am I not?«
God:
»How do you know that it is me, with whom you talk? Let us presume you were telling your psychiatrist, that you had a talk with God. What do you think he would say?«
Valerian:
»That depends on the psychiatrist. Since most of them are atheists, he would probably say, that I talked to myself.«
God:
»Well, he would be right.«
Valerian:
»If you do not mind, would you say you are not?«
God:
»You have this strange capability to come to the wrong conclusions.
Only because you are talking to yourself, I should not exist?«
Valerian:
»Yes. If I thought to talk with you but in reality talked only with myself, in which sense would you exist then?«

God:

»Your question is based on two errors and confusion as well. Your asking if you are you talking with me or not has absolutely nothing to do with the other one, if I do exist or not. Even if you did not now have a discussion with me, though you do have, this does not mean, that I do not exist.«

Valerian:

»Of course, you are right. Instead of commenting 'in case I talk to myself, you do not exist', I should have stated: 'in case I talk to myself, it is clear, that I do not talk to you.«

God:

»Well, quite a different statement from the previous one, but still wrong.«

Valerian:

»Please, If I were only talking to myself, how could I talk to you?«

God:

»How highly irritating, that you must use the word 'only'. I could name you several logical conditions, where it would be possible to talk to yourself, and it would not mean that you did not talk to me.«

Valerian:

»Just give me one.«

God:

»Well, one of them will be met if you and I are the same.«

Valerian:

»Such a thought would be blasphemy- at least if I had said so.«

God:

»According to some religious doctrines that would be the case. According to other statements this is the plain, simple and directly envisioned truth.«

Valerian:

»The only way to end this dilemma for me is to believe, that you and I, we are identical?«

God:

»Not at all. That was only one way out. There are others, of course. For example it could be, that you are a part of me. In this case you would hold conversation with a part of me, that

is you. Or maybe I am a part of you. In that case you would talk with the part that is me. Or you and I, we overlap each other, in which case you would converse with the common being, and logically at the same time with me and yourself. The only
condition where your conversation with yourself could implicate, that you are not talking with me, would mean, that we are absolutely divided from each other, and even then it would be possible that you were talking to both of us at the same time.«

Valerian rather confused and irritated:
»So you state, that you exist.«
God:
»*Not at all. You are coming to the wrong conclusions again. The question of my existence has not even been touched yet. All I said was, that from the simple fact that you are talking to yourself, no one can deduct, that I do not exist, not to forget the simple truth, that then you could not be talking to me.«*
Valerian:
»I concede the point. What I would really like to know is: do you exist?«
God:
»*What a strange question!«*
Valerian:
»Why? People have been asking that same question for thousands of years.«
God:
»*I do know they did. It is not the question that is strange. It is strange that you are posing it.«*
Valerian:
»Why?«
God:
»*Because I am the one whose existence you doubt. I understand your concern. You are afraid, that your present experience with me might be a hallucination. How can you expect to get reliable information from the being about its existence, when you suspect that it is not?«*

Valerian:
»You do not want to tell me, do you exist or not?«
God:
»*I am not stubborn. I just want to explain to you that no answer that I could give you, would satisfy you. Now, if I said: 'No, I do not exist!' What would that prove?*
Absolutely nothing. If I tell you: Yes, I do exist! Would that convince you? Of course not.«
Valerian:
»Now, if even you cannot tell me if you are or not, who then could?«
God:
»*Nobody can tell you. You have to find out yourself.*«
Valerian:
»*That is not what I said. I said: There is no possibility to tell you. But that does not mean that it is impossible to help you.*«
Valerian:
»How could you help me?«
God:
»*In mysterious ways I can send signals to your wounded heart. May be you find a new hope. You hear the song of a bird or see a laughing child. May be you hear a melody, that was lost for years. You can feel the warmth of the sun on your face. You can see the reflection of light in a sparkling drop of water. Your tormented heart is invited to beat again in peace and tranquillity. I am alive, I am the one who watches, I am the fullness of energy and in continuous movement. Just flow along in this living river.*
I send lots of signals to your awareness.
In this way can you get to know me. Your best experience will be, when you can feel, that your mind is linked with mine. This mental nudging can be felt in strange ways by help of other humans or in magic places. You should be prepared to believe in these mental signals.«
Valerian:
»Why is it so difficult for me to accept help from others?«
God:
»*You did not learn to accept the kindness of others as an*

Indication of my presence. As long as you cannot do that, you will not be able to accept help from others.«
Valerian:
»Dear God, I do not know how to go about it. I will try, but I do not know, if I will succeed. When I have found the right way, you will let me know. And if I choose the wrong path, then let me know as well.«
God:
»I propose, you leave that to me. We got astray from our topic anyway. I would like to return to the question, why I gave freedom of will, according to your opinion.
Your first thought, that I gave you a free will in order to test if you are worthy of salvation or not, will be pleasing to a lot of moralists. But I loath that way of thinking. Can you not think of a more friendly, a more human cause, why I gave you a free will?«
Valerian bowed his head, pondered this for a moment and said: »Some time ago I asked an orthodox rabbi this question. He said, that we humans, as we are, cannot simply be happy to get salvation, if we do not feel that we have to earn it. Therefore, in order to merit salvation, we need the freedom of will.«
God:
»This explanation is already more beautiful, than the previous one, but still far beyond the truth. According to the orthodox Jewish faith I made the angels, and they do not have a free will. 'They are seeing me forever.
They are totally immersed in goodness, never do they feel the least temptation towards evil.
They really do not have a free choice. They enjoy eternal bliss, though they never did anything to earn it.' Now, if the explanation of your rabbi is true, why then did I not make angels only but humans as well?«
Valerian:
»I could not say. Why did you?«
God:
»This explanation is incorrect. First of all, I never made instant angels.
All feeling beings are striving towards a final state you could

call 'angelic'. As humans at this level undergo a certain process of biological development, so are the angels the result of a cosmic process of development. The only difference between the so called blessed ones and the so called sinners is, that the blessed are an older species than the latter.
Unfortunately countless cycles of life are necessary to learn the most important fact of the universe - to be evil means pain. All the arguments of moralists, all the so called reasons, why humans should not commit bad deeds, they all come down to nothing in the light of the fundamental truth that being evil means suffering. My dear friend, I am no moralist.
I am totally utilitarian.
That humans like to see me in the role of a moralist is one of the tragedies in human history.
My task in this cosmic plan, if I may use this deceptive word, is not to reward or to punish, but to foster the process, whereby all feeling beings may achieve blissful perfection.«

Valerian:
»Why do you call it deceptive?«
God:
»*What I told you can be deceptive in two ways. First of all my task in the cosmic plan was not properly defined. I am the cosmic plan. It is misleading to talk about it in this way as if I fostered the process by granting enlightenment to feeling beings. I am the process. The ancient sages were near to the truth when they spoke of me as the one who was nothing and everything happening at the same time. In modern language, I am not the cause of the cosmic process.*
I am the process of the universe.
At their present level of development humans could best understand the simple notion that I am the process of inspiration and enlightenment.
Those who want to have a concept of the devil as well should perceive him as the fatal period of time the process takes in the making. In this sense the devil is necessary. The process takes a huge amount of time and here I cannot change a thing. Once the process has been understood, then I can assure you this

painful period will not be understood any more as an inevitable interference or something evil. It will be seen as a part of the process itself.
I know, for you drifting in the woeful sea of mortality, this can not give you full consolation. You might be astonished that when at last you have learned to see the facts from your new perspective, that your short suffering will diminish until at last it will be no more.«

Valerian:
»I have been told that already and I think I will believe it. If I could really look at events with your perspective, I might be happier. But would I not also have responsibilities towards others?«

God laughing:
»You remind me of a mortal who said that he would not enter nirvana until he could see that also all other feeling beings could go there. So everybody waits for someone else to be the first. No wonder it takes them so long. Mortals succumb to another error. He or she believes that they cannot assist others to get salvation. Each person has to do that for himself totally alone. And so everyone strives only for personal salvation.
This alienated attitude towards others makes salvation impossible. To tell the truth, salvation is partly a personal and partly a social process. It is a grave error to believe that when you have achieved enlightenment, you are then exempt from the process and free from the task you help others.
The path where you can help others starts only after you began to see the light!«

Valerian, moaning:
»Dear God, there is something highly irritating in the way you speak of yourself. You state, that essentially you are a process. This makes you seem rather impersonal. But I would like to feel that there is a personal God.«

God:
»Since you need a personal God you deduct that I am he?«

Valerian:
»Not quite. In order to be acceptable for a mortal his faith has to satisfy the needs of this mortal.«

God:
»I understand. But the so called personality of a divine being exists more in the eyes of the believer, than being part of the being himself. The spirited discussions on the question if a am a personal or an impersonal entity are really quite stupid. None of the two is right. From one point of view I am personal, from another I am impersonal. It is the same with humans.
A being from another planet might regard them quite impersonal, an agglomeration of atomic particles, behaving according to strict physical rules. Such a being would have no more interest for the personality of a human being, than the normal man has for an ant.
Knowing that all, for me an ant can have as much personality as a human being. Impersonal attitude is no more right or wrong than the personal one. In general the more we get to know the individual, the more it achieves personality. To put in plainly: do you see me as personal or an impersonal being?«
Valerian:
»Well, I am talking to you, or not?«
God:
»If you look at it this way one could say it is a personal attitude. From another less valid point of view it could also be seen as impersonal.«
Valerian:
»If you are really something as abstract as an ongoing process, I do not see any sense in talking to a simple process.«
God:
»How vexing of you to use the word simple. At the same time you could say that you live in a simple universe. Besides, why should everything have a meaning? Does it make sense to talk with a tree?«
Valerian spontaneously:
»Naturally not.«
God:
»But children and primitives do it at all times.«
Valerian:
»But I am not a child nor am I a primitive.«

God:
»Unfortunately I noticed.«
Valerian:
»Why unfortunately?«
God:
»Because children and primitives do have the natural understanding, that you and the likes of you have lost long ago. Honestly I believe it would do you good to talk to a tree from time to time. It would be more fruitful than talking to me. But we digress from our topic. One last time I would like to come to an understanding, why I gave you a free will.«

Let me remain with the question

Valerian relieved and full of joy confesses:
»All this time the question has been in my mind.«
God:
»Does that mean that you did not pay attention to our conversation?«
Valerian:
»Of course not. But on another plain the question occupied my mind.«
God:
»Did you come to any result?«
Valerian:
»Well, you did say this does not mean a sort of test, if we are worthy of salvation. You did deny that the cause of this was, that humans have to have the feeling that they did earn something in order to enjoy it.
And you stated that you are a utilitarian. But mainly you seemed quite happy when I found out, that not sin is the worst of things, but mostly the sorrow it causes.«
God:
»Quite so. What else could be the worst about sin?«
Valerian:
»Now, you do know this and me as well. But all my life until now I have been under the influence of moralists and they stand for the point of view, that sin itself is the worst. However, if I put together all these informations, I have to presume that the only cause why you gave me the freedom of will, is your conviction, that with their free will humans will cause less hurt to others and to themselves because of that free will.«
God:
»Very nice, until now that has been the best cause you stated. Rest assured that if now I had the choice to grant a free will to you or not, this would have been the decisive argument to give it to you.«

Valerian:
»What does this mean was it not within your power to grant us freedom of will?«

God:
»My dear, to give freedom of will is not due to my arbitrariness as the equal angles of an equilateral triangle could not be arbitrary.«

Valerian:
»And here I thought you could do anything you wanted.«

God:
»Everything logically possible. Did not Holy Thomas Aquinas say: 'It is a sin to regard the fact that God cannot do something impossible as a limitation of his almightiness'. I would agree, but only by substituting the word error for the word sin.«

Valerian:
»That may be, but I am still astonished about your comment that it was not your decision to give me a free will.«

God:
»The time has come to tell you that this entire discussion was based on a huge error from the start. We held this talk under the wrong presumption that we treat a purely ethical problem. You complained in the beginning, that I gave you a free will. You asked the question, if I did right in doing so. You never imagined that the whole affair was not for me to judge.«

Valerian:
»Now I am completely lost.«

God:
»Well, you only regarded the case from a moralistic point of view. You never considered the fundamental metaphysical aspects of the problem.«

Valerian:
»I still do not understand where you want to lead me.«

God:
»Before you asked me to take away your freedom of will, you should have pondered the question of you really have a free will.«

Valerian:
»I took this for granted.«
God:
»*By right of what ?*«
Valerian:
»I do not know. Do I have a free will?«
God:
»*Yes, you do.*«
Valerian:
»Why then did you mention that I should not have taken it for granted?«
God:
»*This was not permitted. Just because incidentally something is true, does not lead to the conclusion that one could presume it to be true.*«
Valerian:
»In any case it is good to know that my conviction to have a free will, was not an error. Sometimes I was concerned that the determinists could be right.«
God:
»Well they are.«
Valerian:
»Now what. Do I have a free will or not.«
God:
»*I told you already that you have it. But this does not mean that the determinists are not right.*«
Valerian:
»Are my actions determined by natural law or are they not?«
God:
»*The word 'determination' is misleading here in a subtle and effective way. In the discussions about the contradictions of freedom of will against determinism this leads to a lot of confusion. Your actions are doubtless in harmony with the natural law, but if you say they are determined by natural law this will give a totally wrong impression. As if your will had the possibility to counteract the natural law, as if nature could be stronger that you and would 'determine' your actions, regardless if you wanted that or not.*

Indeed it is impossible for your will to come into conflict with the law of nature.
You and the law of nature, in reality, you are one.«

Valerian:

»What do you mean that I cannot come into conflict with the law of nature. If I take a hardliner position and decide not to become subject to natural law. What should deter me? If I am determined enough not even you could hinder me.«

God:

»You are quite right. I could not hinder you, nothing could. It will not be necessary to do so, because you could not even start to begin. Remember, what Goethe wrote about nature: 'We obey nature's rules, even if we contradict them, we work together with nature, even when we want to work against her.'
Can you not understand that the so called natural laws are just the description of the ways how you and other beings are acting? They are describing how you are acting, but the do not prescribe the way you should act. They are not a power or a force determining or enforcing your actions. In order to be valid a natural law has to take into account how you want to act or how you will decide to act.«

Valerian:

»You really insist that you will never decide to act against a law of nature?«

God:

»Interesting that you talk of determination with 'being' and not of 'having' it. The synonym is often used. Most people say 'I am determined to do this or that' what they mean is 'I took the decision to do this or that'. This psychological equivalent should demonstrate that determination and free choice are apparently quite near to each other. You could say that the doctrine of the free will teaches that it is you who determines the action. In contradiction the deterministic theory says that your actions are determined by something outside of yourself.
Mostly this difficulty is caused by the fact that you divide reality into a 'you' and a 'not-you'.
Do tell me honestly where exactly are your borders and where does the rest of the universe begin?

Or does the rest of the universe end and you are now beginning? When you start to comprehend the so called 'You' and the so called 'nature' as a continuous entity, then such questions as if it is you ruling nature or rather if nature rules you, will not disturb your tranquillity. Then all the confusion about freedom of will set against determination will ebb away. I will give you a metaphor. Imagine two bodies, moving towards each other because of the attraction force.

If they are feeling beings, each of them will ask the question if it is him or the other exercising the force of attraction. In a certain sense it is them both. And in another sense it is none of them. Best to state that it is the configuration that counts.«

Valerian raised his head, lowered it again and shut his eyes.

»A short while ago you told me that our debate was based on an immense error. You did not tell me what the error was.«

God:

»Well, it was your idea that I had the possibility to create you without a free will. You presumed that this had been a real possibility, equal to the one that I gave you the will to live. You asked yourself, why I did not make another choice. Did it never occur to you that a feeling being is inconceivable without a free will, like a physical object without the force of attraction. Besides there are more similarities between the physical object exerting the force of attraction and a feeling being exerting freedom of will that you could imagine. Honestly you should have great difficulties in imagining a being having awareness without a free will. How in heaven

should it get along? What led you astray is the fact that you have been told that it was me who gave humans a free will. That looks as if I first created man and later on gave him the special gift of a free will. In this case you presume that I own a box of gifts handing out freedom of will to some beings and not to others. The free will is not an addition it is a constitutional part of awareness.

A being with awareness with a free will is metaphysical nonsense.«

Valerian:
»If this is the truth, why did you discuss the matter, which I thought to be a moral problem, all this time with me, just to state finally that my mistake was a kind of metaphysical error.«

God:
»I thought this a good therapy to clean your system from the moralising poison. Most of your mistakes are caused by wrong ideas about morals. Therefore these had to be treated first. Now we have to part. If you need me again, just call me. I am convinced that our meeting will give you strength for quite a long time. But do not forget what I told you about the trees. You need not talk to them a lot if you think that stupid. But you can learn a lot from them, from the rocks and rivers and other creatures of nature. To get rid of your sickly notions of
'sin', 'freedom of will' and 'ethical responsibility' there is nothing better than to turn to a naturalistic view of the world. In certain historical periods such philosophies were quite useful. I am talking of the times when cruel tyrants ruled. If at all, they could only be kept at bay by fear of hell. Since then humankind got a bit wiser. They do not need this terrifying picture of hell any more. Maybe it will help you when I cite to you the words of the great Zen poet Seng Ts'an:*

*'When looking for the pure truth
Do not search for right and wrong,
Squabbling over right and wrong
Is a sickness of the mind'.«*

Slowly and in a soft and kind voice God continued:
»*I can see in your face that these words do console you but they also evoke fear. What are you afraid of?
Do you fear that in your mind you could loose the difference between right and wrong and thus increase the probability of doing wrong?
Do you truly believe that the so called moralistic humans, when practical life is at stake and not just theory, would act*

less ethical than the moralists? Of course not. Most people admit, that even those showing an amoral attitude in theory, will act in a highly ethical way in practical life. Moralists are astonished, that these people show excellent behaviour even without ethical doctrines. They can not imagine that the absence of moralistic principles leads to the prospering of doing good without hindrance. Is the saying that 'squabbling over right and wrong is a sickness of the mind' so very different from the tale about the garden Eden and the fall into sin of Adam, who ate the fruit from the tree of knowledge? The knowledge was the recognition of ethic principles, not of ethical feelings, these feelings Adam owned already. A lot of truth is hidden in this story, although I never forbade Adam to eat the apple. I just counselled him to avoid it. I did tell him it would not do him any good. If he had listened to me he could have saved himself a lot of trouble. He thought to know better. I do wish that theologians would learn at last that I did not punish Adam for his deed, but that the fruit itself was poisonous and that the poison is effective through generations still. Now I really have to go. I do hope that our conversation has freed you to some extent from your sickly morality and gave you a strong orientation towards nature. Remember the good words spoken long ago by Lao-tse, at the time when I took Confucius to task because of his moralistic attitudes.«

'All this talk about the good and the duty,
These endless pricks of the needle make a nervous reader -
Better to seek the cause
Why heaven and earth move on their eternal path,
Why sun and moon keep their light,
Why stars take their ordained place,
Why birds and animals stick with their herds,
And bushes and trees do not move from their soil.
This you shall learn,
To move your steps by inner force,
To follow the path set by nature's law,
Then you will stop To run around diligently
Proclaiming the good and the duty.

The swan need not bathe daily To keep its whiteness.'
Valerian:
»One can see, you prefer the wisdom of the East.«
God:
»Not quite. Some of the most beautiful thoughts come from your native Europe. Did not a certain Wolfgang von Goethe say that 'nothing is as great as nature.' 'We should talk less and do more drawings. For my part I would prefer to cease talking and speak in pictures as living nature does[4].

The fig tree over there, this little snake, the cocoon on the rock quietly awaiting its future, they all are significant signatures; the one who would read their true significance he could dispense with the written word quite soon. The more I think about it, there is a lot of vain idleness, not to say dandyism in talking, then when confronted with the magnificence of an old mountain, the rocky walls of a quiet valley one is standing in silent awe before the grand solemnity of nature'.«

---

[4] Compare with: Raymond M. Smullyan 'the Tao is silent'

CHAPTER III

Valerian has no face

The mortal one was lost in thought while strolling up and down along the rocky banks of the river. He did not want to stop yet he could not decide where to go. He had no aim. He saw many paths. Incertitude held him, where lay the path where he would find fulfilment of his life, the meaning of it all. He was filled with the thought that this could only be a dream, or may be he was only the dream of his body. 'Am I just a body of imagination? Even when I concentrate I have no feeling that indicates if I am awake or dreaming. I am dismayed and the bewilderment seems to confirm that I am dreaming.'

Then Valerian pondered the idea that may be he was a figure of someone else's dream. This perturbed him even more and he asked himself 'why not? Could I not have a dream concerning a person that is me, but whose experiences are parts of the dream that I had myself?'

He did not know how to answer that sort of question.

He had been created. He became a being. That left the question, if he had become a part of reality. As spontaneous as the thought occurred he also asked himself:

'Are the higher animals capable to feel themselves as part of a special species? Was a dog capable of thinking: 'I bet I am looking like that dog over there....'

The monotonous answer remained: 'There can be no dream without the dreamer dreaming it.'

The name Valerian was sufficient.

Could someone deny there was a person named Valerian? How to justify the contradiction than by assuming that Valerian is a person, made real by activity and the ability to perform? Thus we approach the matter.

Valerian is a dream in a dream.

So he existed. In the beginning be thought that to exist without freedom would be the felicity of his being.

Soon he got tired from walking along the rocks. He sat down on a stone on the river bank. When he felt thirsty he crouched down towards the river. The mortal one saw his reflection in the water. In sudden recognition he told himself: 'I do not have a head.'

He constantly pondered the question 'What am I?'

The fact that he had crossed the wilderness by chance, climbed across the rocks and arrived at the river had nothing to do with the discovery that he could not see his face, could not see his head.

It was a quiet and clear day, and the view of the mountain ridges confronting him, rising up across misty valleys down to the majestic river formed a spectacular background.

Then something quite simple happened, he ceased to think.

A strange silence, a weird kind of wakeful limpness and numbness overcame him. The mind, the imaginations, the mental babbling all went quiet.

He could not find his voice. The past, and the future were left behind.

He forgot all the silent questions about who and what he was, his name, his being human, being a live creature, everything one could call existence.

He felt as if born anew in this moment, entirely and unconditionally new, free of all remembrances. There was only the now, the everlasting moment and the clearly seen present.

He had only to look about him. What he saw were two legs in trousers of bright linen, two feet in sandals, shirt sleeves of bright cotton ending in two brown hands, the cotton shirt open at the top end ending in nothing, there was absolutely nothing to see.

This nothing, this hole where the head should be, was no normal empty space, no clear nothing.

Quite the contrary, this space was quite full of everything.

This encompassing emptiness was a space where there was room for grass, trees, the misty hills across and the mountain peaks far away, their snowy ranges resembling white clouds in the sky.

He had no head, only a place wherein the whole world was reflected.

The discovery took his breath away, so engulfed was he in this presence.

The overwhelming scenery, bright and shining in the pure air, was here just being, without any foundation, mysteriously floating in empty space. This lovely scenery and this astonished him, was entirely free from himself, free from any spectator. Its total presence equalled his total absence of body and soul. It was lighter than air, more transparent than glass, entirely free from him.

This vision was no dream, no esoteric revelation, in spite of its magical uncanny appearance. Quite the contrary.

It felt like a sudden awakening from the sleep of normal life, like the end of a dream. It was a self illuminating reality, cleansed from any obscure darkness of the mind.

A revelation of the truth. A moment of light in the mysterious story of his life.

He could no longer ignore something he had been to busy to realize. This was the naked, uncritical recognition of a fact that had been before his eyes all the time, the total absence of a face.

Now everything was simple, clear and understandable, no explanation, no thoughts, no words were necessary.

No questions arose, there was no need above this experience, he felt only peace and a quiet joy and that he had been freed of an enormous burden.

When the first exultation of this revelation settled, he started to discuss it with himself and said: 'One way or the other I vaguely imagined myself as a human being, living within this house, my body, and looking out at the world from the two windows, my eyes.

Now I find that is not quite so. In this moment when I look into the distance how can I know how many eyes I have, two, or three or maybe hundred or none at all?

In reality in this my façade there is only one window visible, and this window is wide open without a frame and nobody is looking out. It is always this other one, he who has eyes and a face to be in the framework, but this one never..... ...

There are two types, two entirely different types of humans, one kind in countless examples, evidently carries a head on its shoulders, a sort of hairy ball with a diameter of two spans and several orifices. The other kind of whom I know only one species, has no such thing on his shoulders.

And I did not realize this important difference. I have been the victim of an illness of the mind, a long hallucination. I always thought myself to be as other humans, but never anticipated to be a living faceless two legged being.

I have been blind for the one ever present fact, the one without I would have rested in blindness, that I have a wonderful substitute of a head, this endless clarity, this brilliant and pure emptiness, which does not hide the entirety of all that is, but is entirety itself.

Where ever I look, I cannot find something like an empty canvas. There is no projection of these mountains, this sun and this sky. There is no mirror to give the reflection.

There is nothing in between, not even the incomprehensible hindrance they call distance. The immense blue sky, the mountain peaks in their rose light, the sparkling green of the grass, how can it all be distant, when there is nothing it could be distanced from?'

With a sigh Valerian breathed so heavily that it hurt and continued to talk to himself:

'Oh Lord, this headless emptiness has no definition and no localisation:

It is not round, or small or large, it is not even here, contrary to being there.

All this colourful contours are perfectly present, without any implications; they are neither far nor near, neither this or that, mine or not mine, perceived by me or just in existence. All doubts, every dualism between subject and object has disappeared.

The more the day advances the more he moves off from the living original.' This was the vision Valerian experienced. At last he had to recognize that it was impossible to cease thinking for a longer period. He thought it was inevitable to make the effort of finding a connection between the enlightened moments of life and the misty plane where they occurred. His sound human sense started to raise objections he could no longer ignore. 'These are experiences', he told himself, 'they will give me something or take something away.
Experience builds proof.' Thus he found his first objection. 'Maybe my head is missing, but not my nose.
Well, here it is, it precedes me, and I can see it, wherever I go...' He had to answer himself: 'If these misty, rose-colored and at the same time quite transparent cloud that is hanging to my right side and the similar cloud, that is hanging to my left are both noses, then I count two of this sort and not one. And the quite solid hump I can see in other faces, is therefore then no nose. Only a hopelessly mendacious and confused observer would choose the same name for so different objects. I prefer to believe in an encyclopaedia and the common custom, and they force me to admit, that nearly all human beings do have one nose per person; but I do not have one. What would happen... if some erring over-zealous sceptic would like to plant me a facer in this location, he would aim right between these two rose coloured clouds! The result would be as unpleasant as if I owned the most solid nose, made for boxing. What happens to these multiple subtle tensions, feelings, pressure senses, tickling, itching and feelings of pain, that always happen in this central area?
How is it with the tactile sensitivity, when I place my hand there? In the end all the facts give me the overwhelming proof that my head is existing here and now, or does it not?' Valerian sighed aloud, stretched his arms wide and opened his hands as if to present his thoughts in their palms.
'Without a doubt', he exulted, 'without any doubt there exist many sensations one cannot ignore, but out of them you cannot make a head or something similar to a head.

The only way to make a head out of them would be to collect all the necessary ingredients that are missing, especially the three dimensional colourful forms. What kind of head is this, who has countless perceptions, but the bodily organs like eyes, ears, mouth, hair seemingly do not exist here as according to observation all other heads do have them.

Fact is that this location has to be kept free from all obstacles, from every whiff of mist or coloration that could obscure my universe. However, if I start now to search about for my lost head, I will not find it but may loose the searching hand as well. The hand will also be devoured by the abyss in the centre of my being. Oh, my God!' he moaned quite desperate. 'A long time ago, when I had been dreamed, the sun high in the sky woke me up.

I saw a far away cloud on a mountain range, light as a bird. Then the sky erupted in colours. A column of fire surrounded the temple and the ring of flames tightened.

The thought arose to flee into the water; but I approached the rings of fire and they caressed me and covered me like a flood without heat and burning. With relief I recognised that I had been dreaming. Or did someone else dream me?'

And here and now he told himself: 'Evidently this gaping hole, this empty base of all my operations, this magical place where I thought to have my head resembles a beacon of light. The fire burns with such heat that everything getting within its circle is devoured instantly and totally. Because of its brightness and force my world can never fall into darkness, not for a single moment. As for the so called itching or feelings of pain, they cannot extinguish this central fire, as even these mountains, the clouds or the sky could extinguish it, quite the contrary.

They all exist in a light and through the light one can see the brightness. Present experience,' he told himself, 'takes place only in an empty and absent head, never mind what sense one is using for it.

Because here and now my world and my head exclude each other. They are not compatible.

There is no place on my shoulders for both of them. Unfortunately it seems to be my head with all his anatomy which had to cede. I do not need proof to see this I am not required to find a special state of mind, I need only the ability to see, the power to state: 'See who is here,' - instead of a 'just think who is here.' If I am not capable to see what I am, or what I am not, because I am overburdened with imaginations, too caught in spirit to accept the situation as I find it at this moment. My head is just a fixed idea, as are my face and my eyes. The truth is, to speak with the wise ones, only you my God can see everything, hear and live everything.' Valerian found this recognition in no way satisfactory.

Standing on the rocks

Valerian felt better and safer, in a certain sense even stronger. The exultation he felt when his thoughts were formed declined only when he formed words and spoke them. 'Probably there is only one way to get information on my nature. I will ask God. I will implore him to look at me and give me his true opinion.' "God", he shouted right away. Then he continued in a soft voice: "Dear God, it is said that you created all humans, because it is written: *'Let Us make man in Our image, according to Our likeness; and so God created man in His own image; as male and female He created them.*
Then God blessed them' (1.Mose 1,26)."
God:
"And I looked at all that was made, and I saw that it was good."
Valerian:
"I do not have a head."
God:
"Of course you have a head."
Valerian:
"If I had a head, then there would be a face, then I would have eyes and a sound human intelligence. But I am talking to you and cannot see you."

God:
"You can see me."
Valerian:
"How for heaven's sake can I see you?"
God:
"There are different sorts of explanations. The truth is, the verb 'to see' has two quite contradictory meanings. When you observe two people who are talking to each other, then you know that they see each other.
Their faces are unchanged and they talk at a distance of about one meter. But when I see you, then your face is everything, and mine is nothing. Because seeing is not only the closed chain of physical processes, whereas light waves pupils, maculae, the visual centre and a part of the brain are needed, so that scientists cannot find a missing link.
What I mean is the seeing without eyes. I see with my spirit."
Valerian, quite sceptical:
"I am a human being. Should I deduct from the fact that you have no head, that I also have none?"
God:
"You should be ashamed of yourself, to utter such an idea."
Valerian sat on the river bank quite subdued and did not dare to look into the water. He tried to look into his own body, tried to see his own heart beat.
Then God spoke to him again:
"You are human, in spite of the radical differences between you and all the other beings of your species."
Valerian:
"Then I am a mortal."
God:
"You think in the way a child does. You are seeing things outside yourself, who have something in common as their appearance, their behaviour and you think that they all could include you.
You ask yourself: how would it be if I was part of them? You catch only a part of the entire picture, this one has feet, I have feet, that one has hands, I have hands …… hmmm."
After a moment of silence God continued:

"These partial pictures might lead to an entire effigy.
Thus it happened that you made the deduction: I have no head, therefore you do not have one either, although you can not even see me."
Valerian:
"That leaves me again with the fact that I do not know anything about myself."
God:
"What irritates you are the two different ways one can talk about 'seeing'. When this concerns me it happens quite differently than when it concerns only you."
Valerian:
"How can I see you?"
God:
"You can see me in your own self, in all human beings, in everything that lives and has a soul."
Valerian:
"At first I did not think. I never thought about myself or about what and how I am."
God:
"I presume there is a way to convince you that you have got a head. Possibly you have a thorough though vague foreboding of your true being.
After a time you will be convinced that a self-centered egotistic contemplation is nonsensical, maybe you had a vision or you were immersed in a dream of your own self.
In ancient times of life on earth humans often had visions and cults where loose and flying heads played a role, visions of one eyed or headless monsters and ghosts, of human bodies crowned by animal heads, apparitions of beheaded martyrs who walked about and talked. Doubtless quite fantastic images."
Valerian:
"When I can see the head, is it not all the same if I meet him in the form of a donkey's head or a bunch of flowers.
Quite possibly I could have lots of heads, so that I do not even know

what do with them[5].

To give him a proper place, here on my shoulders, where he could fill out the central emptiness,
this emptiness that is my source of life, this could only happen by chance. It is not really important."

God:

"You will learn with experience. Do not trouble yourself, all these peculiarities are part of your personality. Some time in the future logic will prevail over intuition."

Valerian:

"Do I have a brain? Will I really die? How will that feel?"

God:

"Spare me the answers to these questions. You have been thinking about them a lot and you will continue to do so quite often in your life. You will have to accept that your existence has only a certain degree of infinity. You can choose. Now you are swaying between a subjective and an objective view of the world, and this difficult position is an essential part of human nature. And now I have to say good bye."

---

[5] Cerpts from D. E. Harding's 'On having no Head'.

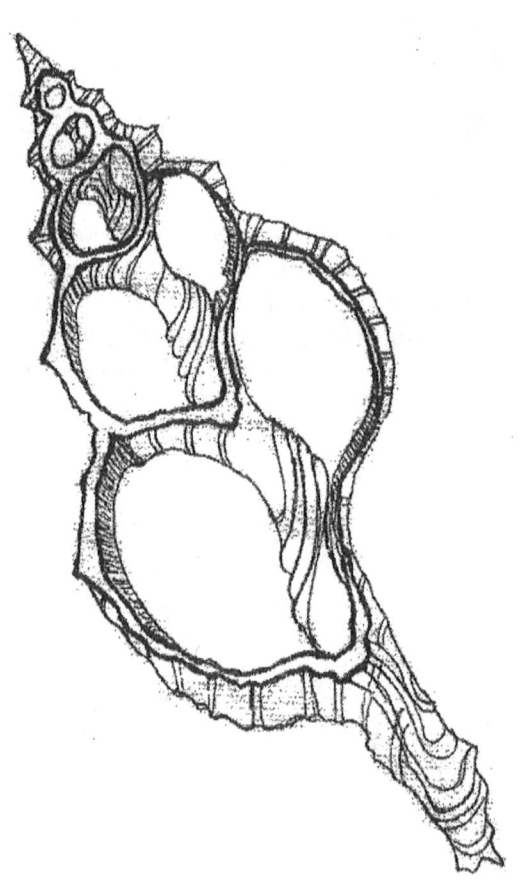

CHAPTER IV

Asking for the right way

Valerian leaned on a tree trunk, he was in no way satisfied and he spoke slowly and in a clear voice:
"Dear God, wherever you are now, we will talk to each other. I know, you will answer all my questions in your own very special way. Nothing remains without an answer in your time. There are still some puzzles not solved, that prevent my moving on. In the meantime I also know that you did not leave me, because at the beginning you said that you are present always and everywhere, that you are alive behind me, before me, besides me and within me. So how could you desert me?"
God:
"I give you time to think."
Valerian:
"I will do that later, when you have taught me to be patient. For now please tell me why did you counsel me in the beginning to talk with a tree? I have learned that in the book Deutero-Isaiah accuses the worshippers of trees that they take a piece of wood for a god. The ancient Germanic tribes worshipped the tree of the world, risen from a root that should remain hidden from mankind.
This is too difficult and complicated for me. I think that the wonderfully spread network of branches gives a fair comparison with the network of the order of the universe."
God:
"You've nearly hit it."
Valerian, quite happy:
"Am I right?"
God:
"I did not say that. I just wanted to state, that I agree with your phrasing. See, in the cross of Jesus the wood of the tree was the symbol for the order of the new saved world.
'Ecce lignum crucis in quo salus mundi pependit'."

Valerian:
"I do understand. Although in the ancient times of the church the cross was the symbol of the Christian faith, it had quite another form, the 'crux quadrata', a cross with four arms of equal length. It was considered a holy sign, though never had someone been sacrificed on it."

God:
"Quite right. This was the symbol of the arbour of the world. You can find the cosmic cross of coordinates in any compass. Later on it became a Christian symbol, since Christ is the real arbour of this world. He was born into this world into the axle of this world, and tied to the tree of suffering. Therefore and only therefore the ancient salvation symbol of the cross could be understood by Christendom as the symbol of Jesus Christ, the symbol of forgiving love."

Valerian stood away form the tree trunk and walked to the river bank where he knelt and clung with his hands to the rocks at the river bank and whispered faintly: "This means that we have to endure life as it is given to us and the world as it is, and that we have to endure our own self and also all the other humans around us."

God:
"Suffering and love are part of the life of every human being. Pontius Pilatus did not know what he meant, when he pointed at my beaten and bleeding son Jesus Christ and said: 'Ecce homo' - 'See, what a man'.

Valerian:
"He spoke words that he himself did not understand?"

God:
"Yes, humans often do not understand their thoughts and their actions. In this words Pilatus spoke of the incomparable example, that the effigy of the sufferer, the loving one, the sacrifice and the sacrificed is the real image of mankind. You have to look at this picture if you want to know what man is."

Valerian lost in thought and restless breathed heavily and tried to arrange his thoughts. Then he hesitantly spoke:
"I wanted to say something quite different and ask quite a different question. It is about the path, which I did not choose,

which nobody chooses, but has to follow it, if he suffers or not. For I think that nobody can determine his own life himself."
God:
"Go ahead."
Valerian:
"During our first talk you spoke of the Tao and of Confucius. In Chinese philosophy the order of all things is named Tao, and Tao means 'the Way'."
God:
"This does not mean a way leading from one place to another, or from one condition to another, this way rather means the sense, the method, the manner in which I am absolutely present. It is the manner how the universe moves, as things appear and disappear quietly in space and time. The wise ones consider Tao as a principle of order, where all contradictions are resolved."
Valerian:
"In the Christian faith this is quite different. You yourself explained to me that 'God is spirit'. I think spirit is nothing immobile, spirit is not rigid, spirit is the way and continuous movement. In my opinion you create a multitude of beings and join them together into the great reality. Biblically your divinity is expressed as the way to diversity, the way of multiplicity."
God:
"The wisdom emanating from me creates the multitude of reality, by my wisdom the created diversity if brought into a meaningful unity. 'I walked around the spheres of heaven and into the depths of the abyss!' From my words you should learn that all the paths on earth lead to the two areas I would like to name nature and history, but also all paths come from me and lead back to me."
Valerian:
"So it is you who decides within history of man the path of every single person?"
God:
"I will be here as the one that is. I go along with humans, but only in the way of my will. This then decides the path of the

humans. My will is done. Remember what has been told about Joseph and his brothers. They decided to kill him after he had told them about his dreams, they were jealous and did not want to give him the honour due to him. The outcome was quite the contrary of what the brothers had intended. Because he had been sold to the Egyptians, he acquired there a post of honour. Then he was able to help his brothers in the time of famine. With their attempt to get him killed, the brothers provided the preconditions for their own dependence. Out of this case the Bible deducts (1. Mose 50:20) *that my ways, seen in their entirety, are woven not by the free will of man, but by my spirit. My intention and the way it works are and remain a secret in the eyes of men. So they call me by my name, the name of God."*

Valerian:
"Thus it makes sense that Joseph said: 'Not you have brought me here, but God.' Something I did learn here, you do not make an appearance in history, but it is you who forms the frame and within this frame the actions of humans take place. Completed actions are like goals reached and different ways lead to each goal."

God:
"The ways have a different significance from the goals. The ladder you use is something different from the roof you ant to reach with its help."

Valerian:
"Well there has to be a difference. When I want to take a wandering, then the wandering itself is the goal. I go this way because it pleases me. I can also run a distance without regarding the way if I want to reach a certain meeting point at a given time. There is a difference between the way and the goal."

God:
"I feel your interest. But remember one truth: Not one single moment in history is there to wait just for another moment. Each one has its own significance, it will remain in my thoughts, even when it has been long lost in mortal time. My aim is not the future of history, every single moment is an

aim for me. Whatever happens here and now is a sort of 'way', for from this moment something new will arise. At the same time it is also a 'goal', for the process of reality has reached in it its place and its final form that can not be changed in eternity. For an example the fact that you are alive."

Valerian spoke slowly and carefully, as if a raised voice could destroy the precious moment.

"I am alive in time. All events follow one another. But a passing moment is short lived. Therefore it is easier for me to talk in pictures. I compare the time according to what is happening, either with a runner, or a crawling animal, or a medicine. All together they do not depict time, but movement, a relation in space. To feel the running of time I use an hourglass. Even if it does not show time it makes me feel how quick or slow, according to my kind of contemplation, the time is passing. I move within living on. I cannot live outside time."

God:

"What you experience can only be your limited periods of time, hours, days, years, your life. But time moves on beyond these limited periods. This is valid for the past and for the future. You can perceive the tightly limited and the vastest extended period of time only as a fragment of a larger horizon of time. The end of time as well as the beginning of time is incomprehensible to you. You can not imagine that there is no before and no thereafter. You can only imagine time as something endless. Me, I know the Beginning and the End. Alpha and Omega."

Valerian, deep in thought:

"That does not astonish me. The endless stream of time is evidently the precondition that I can experience some periods or parts of time at all.

My modest experience with time tells me that there has to exist the idea of an unlimited horizon of time, of eternity."

God kept silence for a while before he spoke reluctantly:

"You are on the right path. For eternity is simply not the same as en endless continuity of periods of time. You should never ask how many seconds eternity has. Eternity is not a passing time, where the single seconds appear and disappear, neither

is it absence of time. Eternity is beyond time. In eternity time does not pass, time in eternity does not flow or run, for eternity is an everlasting now."
Valerian:
"A situation the mind cannot grasp."
God:
"*But everybody desires it.*"
Valerian:
"I live within this time. I live within history. It is the continuation of various periods of time. History connects them. But the future remains open. My present is what humans before me thought of as the future. What I now think of as future, will be the present for other humans.
Salomon said: *'There is a special hour for everything; for every action under the heavens there is a special time.'* This he wrote in his teachings in Chapter 3. *'I know that all that God does is made for eternity. And what is, has existed for a long time, and what will be has also exited long before.'* There is nothing to add here and nothing to omit."
God:
"*Quite right. This makes sense.*
You can see the past clearly only when events in the futures show you, what you achieved in the past. This is valid also for the present. Probably you do not know that I am interested in observing why mortals are acting as they do.
What I do see is that they all are not not able to comprehend the process that evolves under the sun."
Valerian:
"Not to forget the fact that not only good things happened, but that tremendous damages occurred in these long times, caused either by nature or by man.
I am astonished that everything was not lost in chaos."
God:
"*My hands uphold the order of things. I preserve and will keep destruction at bay. I influence the course of history,*
let us say reality as a whole. Nature and the process of history are intertwined. I rule the entirety of reality, because in my eternal presence I see its total complexity."

Valerian:
"If eternity is the fullness of all times, then the essence of life is coming from there. Then eternity rules time and its ending course?"

God:
"*I AM WHO I AM.*" (2. Mose 3:14) *I Am God, the Lord, He Who is, Who was, and will always be." As I see the total process of reality I rule the world by providence: I set the specific goals for all that exists."*

Valerian:
"But the actions of my freedom, of my free will, the things I do as a mortal you can not determine in advance."

God:
"I can not determine them in advance, but I know them from the beginning. I can integrate them into my plan of the world. You can reject a plan you thought up before.

In unerring providence I know what you are doing, what you decline, and what you will decide as a mortal as one living in the present. All that moves in the future I have already seen. With one wink it will forestall your changes and surround them.."

Valerian:
"When we started our talk I did not know anything about the result. I did implore you to take back my free will. I still recognize my complications with the outside world and the uniformity of my inner self.

They can not hold one pace with each other. Other mortals have detected myriads of stars and spiral arms, rotating in the universe in immeasurable distances.

They opened the secret world of atoms and electrons, not less fascinating than the cosmic space.

The human mind explored the farthest past. The process of thinking, which enlightens the

farthest objects, is still obscured for me. I live my own life without giving much thought to laws and causes.

Present happens. The truth remains, that I as a mortal am bound to my time and that I cannot add anything, even should I have found my own way."

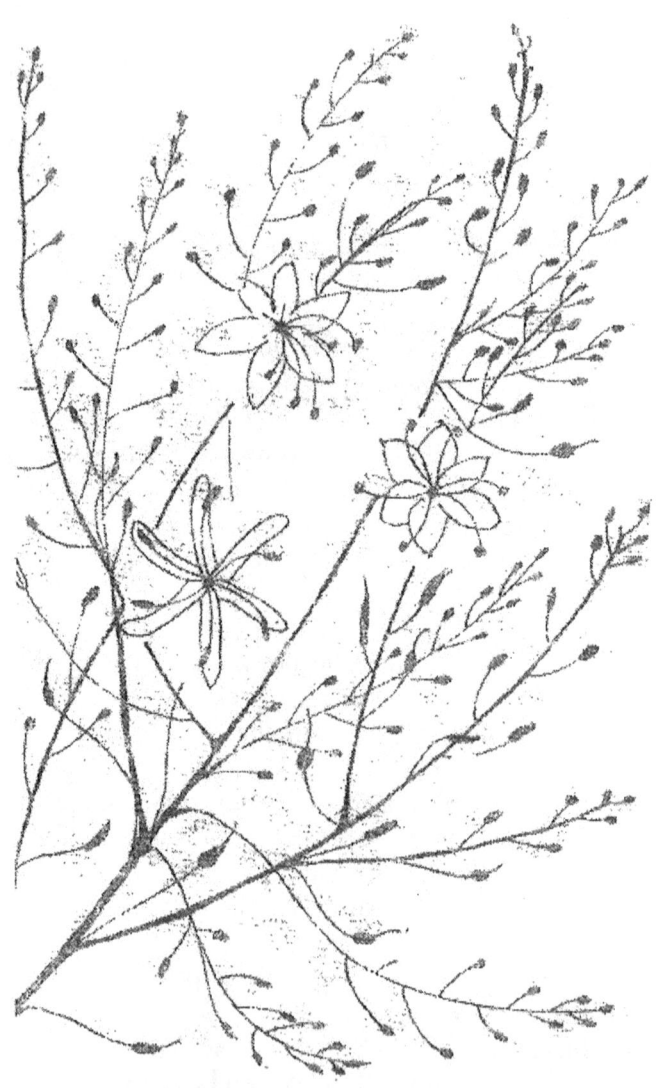

CHAPTER V

Was I made?

Valerian still leaned on the tree trunk and regarded the walls of the temple. He still pondered the same thought.
Even when it extended, he did not follow one branch or another twig, but remained at the root. As before, he talked to himself. 'As many branches as the tree is spreading over me, I cannot put them together, I cannot form a harmonious entirety out of them. How then should I be able to understand anything that is beyond my own being? How should I know what importance this or the other branch or twig does have, when I do not know enough of my own self? I am standing here and I do not know what will happen in this moment that just began? Will I stay standing upright or will I fall down. I did acquire wisdom, more than anybody who was here before me. My heart will strive to find wisdom and to see my own folly. I know, where there is a lot of wisdom there is also a lot of trouble, as Salomon did state already:
'And the sun rises and goes down, moving towards the place where he will rise again. The wind blows to the south and turns north. He takes turns and always returns to his starting point. All rivers fall into the sea and the sea is never filled. The rivers stream towards the place they always sought. The words are difficult to find and there is nothing I can say. The eye does not tire from seeing and the ear not from hearing. What has been is that what will be again. What has been done is that what will be done again.' Salomon asked: *'Is there nothing new?'*
And Valerian asked: 'And what gain do people get from their endeavours? Some time – and only God knows when – everything will be completed. No more questions will be asked.' Something happened.
To Valerian it seemed as if a huge woven cloth was stretched out before him loaded with a heap of puzzle stones.

From these puzzles he should form a picture, a harmonious picture that he did not know yet, a picture without a pattern or an example. He started taking up the first stone and giving it a place on the cloth.

He realized that the stone had four different lateral forms into these the fitting stones out of the pile should be placed.

Now on the spread out cloth lay one point with colours and contours but nothing else. So he took another piece at random out of the pile and placed it along the first one.

Patiently and with great discipline he continued his work.

He changed and put together and he talked to himself, convinced that this would help with the work.

'How difficult to form a complete picture out of these numerous small parts, I will place them around the centre. The first stone is not the beginning, nor will it be the end, but rather the middle. Somewhere in there is also my focus, the point where my life started. I am not looking for my beginning or for my end but for my centre. There is sense in the centre. This centre has edges and angles. Other parts are difficult to add. None of these parts has any force of attraction, or may be they do?'

Valerian then remembered what God had said...... *'did it never occur to you that a feeling being without freedom of will is just as inconceivable as a physical object without force of attraction... not to mention that between the physical object exerting attraction and a feeling being exerting freedom of will, there is a greater similarity than you could perceive'....*

Valerian added thoughtfully:

'A feeling being with a force of will......and a body with attraction, will I ever become something like that? Both in one? When I put a lot of parts of thinking together, right and left from the middle and from start and end?

Where is the start and where is the end? Is my heartbeat the middle between the two? What will happen when attraction is exerted from another middle towards me?

What will happen then?

Valerian felt how his surroundings became clearer and more distinct, how the puzzle formed itself into a picture because he wanted it to, not because he told it how. He had not seen the pattern.

God had told him:

'My dear friend, freedom of will is not a state. It is a fixed part of the innermost core of your consciousness. To be without freedom of will is nonsense.'

Valerian took a break and regarded his work. He thought about the words God had spoken to him and said:

'At the beginning there was the will of the One, the Great One, the entirety. All being is the expression of His Will that means His word. For it is written: 'In the beginning was the Word. And the Word was with God; and the Word was God; He was in the beginning with God; all things were made trough Him and without Him nothing was made. In Him was life, and the life was the light of men' (John.1:1-5).

Valerian sighed and continued his contemplation and he deducted that the absolute, the one truth behind the being, has to be an eternal, ever present, boundless and unchangeable principle. Any contemplation on this subject is impossible.

'My limited mind cannot grasp its sense.

I can only find 'this one force' the essential one, by getting to know life in all its diversity. I can advance with the certainty that this one force exists. This force precedes all things, it is the cause of our being.

All that exists is the result of its work. Therefore nothing can be dead, everything is organic and alive. The entire creation is one living organism. But God not only made the world, he is the spiritual world. All that is, was and will be is eternal, for its basic substance is the same, it is a manifestation of the eternal.'

Valerian sighed aloud.

"My God, you have taught me a lot already, but please tell me, what sort of person am I in your eyes?"

God:

"Are you not content with the knowledge, that a soul is active in your body.

You called it 'your core' yourself and had your heart in mind. The soul is the unseeable core in your being. The soul can see the surrounding world, but it will remain a secret."

Valerian:

"Is there a secret in every living being on this world?"

God:

"Yes. Every being is a secret in itself. But there are living entities who deny having a soul. They live in presuming that their brains are doing all the work. I know that they have no understanding how a brain, made from material only, could achieve something like thinking and feeling.

They are convinced that their unproven statements are highly scientific. This sort of materialism is even more primitive than the most primitive belief in souls. Many renowned philosophers proved the logical impossibility of this theory that persistently cuts off the branch on which it is sitting. They try to prove with the methods of the soul that a soul can not exist."

Valerian:

"It is clear to me that there must be without any doubt a connection between the brain and the knowledge and with the feeling that you summed up with the word soul."

God:

"In no way is the brain substance the same as immaterial feeling and thinking. I know what a complicated, difficult task is it to lighten up the inner world to give it some order; such as you tried with the comparing puzzles. Your mind is first of all oriented towards the outer world.

It is defined to see 'brightness' but not 'the light'. But you can solve the mysteries of the outer world only after you have begun to understand the inner world, where problems are defined and solved.

You long to explore the limits of knowledge, to get to the core of the matter."

Valerian:

"I can see the world, but I have difficulty to understand it."

God:
"Only with the help of my spirit within you, you have the capability to recognize the invisible. You have the physical will and the will of the soul. The will of your soul is stronger than the physical will. Here we find the solution to what you desired at the beginning, you wanted not to have a free will in order to avoid sin."
Valerian:
"Dear God, you mean the will of my body?"
God:
"This will is in conflict with the will of your soul."
Valerian:
"To know these two forces of will, to have deeper knowledge of them, would that be the solution of my problem?"
God:
"Yes, my friend, only this will make you a person and you will find contentment solely, when you can hold these two forces in a healthy and harmonious balance. Then you may be able to aspire to want what you really wish and be in harmony with yourself in your own centre. If you asked me about the best way to achieve getting entrance into your inner life, then I would advise you to start with the natural way. What you experienced yourself you will know best. And if there are moments where you cannot make up your mind about yourself, then meditation will bring you understanding. Tranquillity is the sound of the soul."
Valerian felt upset in the moment he could not hear the voice of God any more. He wanted to call to him 'speak to me', 'please keep talking to me', but he did not say a word and waited.
A question Seneca had posed came to his mind:
'Do you know someone who would know how he came about to desire what he wants? How disgraceful not to walk your own way but to be drawn along and to ask oneself stunned in the middle of the vortex of events 'However did I get here?'
(37,3-5).
'One way leads to me,' he repeated to himself, to memorize it, 'a straight way. There is no way around?'

Valerian was stunned when he heard the voice of God again:
"I Am the whole, the vast ENTITY. I Am not composed of parts. As I Am entirety and perfection, I place varied minuscule particles of my totality in each created living being. I share, and I keep on sharing. I Am not diminished and will not become void. I remain what I was and what I AM and what I will be in eternity.
I Am the One Who is (2.Mose 3:14).
I Am the glass of water from which you drink and that will never be empty. I Am the bread that will nourish you all time. From there all living beings are linked in a spiritual way albeit differing vastly.
They all are a part of the whole.
Since all living beings are linked with Me who made them, they all crave to return to Me. Listen, what Paul, the Roman, wrote:
..'always strive to be reasonable. For as we have many members in one body, but all the members do not have the same function; so we, being many, are one body in Christ, and individually members of one another.
Having then gifts differing according to the grace that is given to us, let us use them' (Rom. 12:4-5)."
Valerian:
"This is all wonderfully complicated. But I am glad to know and to have the capability to understand that all beings do have their own free will. You and I we are an example of this. And within me there is one part having lesser freedom than my physical desire, because it is linked to your spirit.
Am I right?"
God:
"You have it nearly right. At the start you asked the question, if you had the will to commit sin, or not.
I tell you: you are an 'inner' and as well an 'outer' person, both are contending for dominance.
Plainly spoken your forceful outer person tries to dominate your inner person, to ignore its voice, to silence it. But in this process the latter will be victorious."

Valerian:
"I am within a process that means within a movement, within a procedure having its own rules. Did you not say that you are the process."
God:
"Quite so."
Valerian:
"How am I to understand this in this context?"
God:
"I make reality over aeons of time where not one of the particles can move uncontrolled outside the orderly process.
This would lead in the ongoing process to disturbances of the entirety. Every single deviation will be retied by other forces to the total structure of order. All beings have to learn to relate to each other, so that they will not irritate and block each other, but will foster each other and their mutual development. I have made the universe in courses arranged thus that past, present and future form a harmonious entire reality. The setting of each single law of nature is in harmony with my view towards entirety of all times. I keep in mind all those who are no more. It is I who willed every singe being into life, so that every single moment in the history of nature and of man is of spiritual importance. Bluntly spoken mortal minds and earthly matter are manifestations of My Divine Spirit. The Spiritual within material reality means that each being is more than its recognizable existence. Reality itself is a vast continuum of properties and forces. Living beings are for a short while the bearers of this continuity. Continuity is not worn out within the single beings. The direction and order of these forces can never be the accomplishment of a single person, because every single being carries it only within a limited amount of time. My strength determines the reality of the single being as an emanation of my force that permeates and upholds everything. Every mortal being, all activities are reality imbued with the essence of my spirit.
That is why your consciousness has a special character, it reaches beyond yourself, getting a conscious understanding

of many beings in this world. In a mortal way it reflects a sparkle of My Divine Spirit that holds the universe and is ever present."

***

Valerian returned to silence. Not without a certain pride he thought: 'Something is happening within me, in my centre, something that is important. This is not a dream, this is real, I as a single person am important for the entirety. If I were only a piece of a puzzle the picture could not be completed without me, if I were not, something of the total would be missing. In this gigantic puzzle I have my ordained place, where others will be linked with me. This I did find out after I made a lot of errors when putting it together. But I do not know what picture will emerge. I just try to find the connection with my life and the rest of reality. That means also that I have to arrange my way of thinking and acting in applying more energy.
"Dear God, one more question," he pleaded at last.
God:
"Go ahead my friend."
Valerian:
"At first I thought that I could only be a part of the whole if I could define every single action of mine and anticipate which links and interconnections they would have in relation to the entirety of reality. If I had this knowledge then I could not commit any wrong action, for I would know what would happen if I did it and I could deliberate beforehand how to make it work without being noticed."
God:
"You presume that you could be my equal, for only I can see the complete universe. But you do not have my strength.
You cannot know all circumstances encouraging my doings and you cannot comprehend neither for a short period nor for a long one what will be the result of my work."

And Valerian experienced the sufferings of comprehension that the supreme entirety could only be God. More and more he felt his limitations. He knew that he could never uncover the full meaning of his life and of the lives of those who were interwoven in his existence.

He had no key for this special door. The image of the ancient temple from where he came was his hidden secret. There he had been formed by the one who knew and could shape the divine dimensions. He had no recall of this, he only remembered a flash, a hidden awareness of the vast stream of life and its inner connection.

But this light went out immediately and the meaning of life remained obscured. He tried to console himself with the thought that nobody knew the goal and the aim of his life. He had only the possibility to grope about, to pick up something and let if fall again, to stand still or to move around cautiously. From there arose the vexations that caused his confusion. Valerian did not know where he should turn to. He desired freedom, he did not want either insecurity nor confusion. He could only suspect that other possibilities existed. But the true image of himself was hidden from him. Then he asked:

"Dear God, how can I discover in my life my true human nature, when I know that I can never find my self acting personality?"

God:

"*You have to live according to your nature.*"

Valerian:

"What do you mean by that?"

God:

"*Too many things are involved, your understanding is too limited, therefore you can not arrange your formation yourself. As your individual life is interwoven with the entirety that is Me, your realization as a personality can only be assured by Me, since all reality is guided by* Me."

Valerian:

"So you are the cause of all?"

God:

"*Only cause makes sense.*"

Valerian:

"Plato said that there are five causes. He named them: 'W*hat from, where from, where in, what for, why*', and he underlined: '*all this has the One, Who made them, God.*' He is that from which matter was made, the form, the rules, the order."

God:

"*The cause, the reason they form the matter and change it at their convenience.There has to be something in order to become something, and something to make it do so. One is the cause, that other is matter. All art is only imitation of nature. What I said about the universe, I can translate in regard of the task of man. Look at the statue of the tiger above the ancient and ruined door of the temple. The stone has crumbled, but the raw material was there. An artist gave the matter its form. So the statue is the matter, in this case marble, and the cause the artist, the stone mason. The pre-condition for all things is they consist of that what came into existence and the force that works it.*"

Valerian:

"I do understand. The first cause is matter itself, because without matter nothing can be achieved. Then there is the stone mason, who made the work, created the statue. And we have to add the effect that the statue has on me. That is one of its purposes, I presume."

God:

"*You found that marble was the first cause for the statue.*
For it could not have been made, if there had not been matter from which it was cut. The second cause is the artist. He worked the marble, he had trained hands. He gave the stone the form. So the tiger was made. Then we add the cause, the intent. Had there been no intent, then the tiger would not have been made."

Valerian:

"What is intent?"

God:

"*The idea, the artist's motive to make the sculpture. Maybe he earned a lot of money, may be he craved the fame, may be it*

was his devotion that made him create the tiger for the temple."
Valerian:
"The primordial image, which he called idea, was it that where the artist looked when he made it reality. Many causes are causes. But what is THE one cause? The product is a part of the cause, not the cause itself."
God:
"The ongoing influence of reason, naturally. If you want, this means God as a cause without cause."
Valerian:
"Until now I could follow this. But I am also doing something in my life, I can have an effect on things."
God:
"You have your ability to affect things only thanks to my divine force that brought you into being. Your own strength is thus the result of another source, and I am the source."
Valerian:
"My strength is then not my own. When I am my full self I am as well the kind of another. My being me is also the being of some other one, being also you, because you own it. The being of another one is also me. It is a duality."
God:
"This duality is insoluble."
Valerian:
"I can experience independent actions and can know at the same time that my doings are part of your creational activity. And this will go on all the time of my life.

Because, whatever I do will be influenced by circumstances and partly caused by things that happen in the world. I have no means to control these events. So my actions are my doing, but they do also belong to you, my God. You make them possible and you decide their consequences.

There is an indivisible duality in human self assessment.

My actions lead to results that do not belong to me, but will be an emanation of your will, your divine power, they who created me and my action and all other reality out of the void."

God:
"I see that we are beginning to understand each other."
Valerian:
When Goethe described nature as an image and pattern of God, he wrote, '*That all is made in the name of the One who is creation itself*', and also '*that all beings in this world are your image and a metaphor of you.*'
He named each lamp the reflection of some '*higher light*' and the flame the simile. '*As far as ear and eye reach out, I only find familiar things, resembling you.*' Now I want to know, what makes me resembling the divine?"
God:
"You are a 'thought of God', say an image of my thinking, however not in regard of divine eternity."
Valerian:
"Are you forming the structures of nature?"
God:
"The force of nature is always a force of my rule. So to speak, I am the one who forms it."
Valerian:
"There is a tension between the limitless horizon of my thoughts and the limited measure of my form. So is my form corresponding to my being created?"
God:
"My friend, you can call yourself created when you can endure the tension. I mean, if you do not overstep the manifold complicated limited sphere, when you do not enclose yourself stubbornly within the meaningless bustle of life and neglect the wide and ultimate horizons.
If you do all the small tasks of daily life conscientiously and if you remember always that there are vaster horizons than you could envisage, then you are forming a personality."
Valerian:
"In my understanding that means that as a human I can never do all the things offered to me, because then I will do nothing right. But If I do the one thing that I am doing really right, when I know the interwoven and interdependent relations and understand them and take them into account in my actions."

God:
"When you do something the right way you should see the equability of everything that is done the right way."
Valerian:
"That is only possible if I do the one thing that occupies me mostly not detached from the overall purpose, but rather consider it as the point where the vast weavings of the immense universe are working together here and now[6]."
God:
"Only when you fulfil a single task within a multiple horizon, you can complete it reasonably well. Formation is aimed at the single person, but it is always obtained through the boundless horizon of worldly wisdom.

Then your actions will lead to results that are an emanation of the will of my divine power."

---

[6] Extracts from Herbert Huber: 'People, Fable, Myths'.

***

Valerian remained thoughtful. He felt that many things were difficult to understand. But he did not resign and asked another question: "What will it be like, when my everyday life is finished, when it is your will to extinguish my free will?"
God: *"This question is a surprise. We will talk about it later."*
Valerian: "Later, when will it be later? Will my immortal soul, my centre be separated from me, will it leave my body? Will my spirit detach itself from the material form and go back to you, the immeasurable spirit of the universe, the cosmic entirety? Am I right?"
God:
"You want to have it the easy way, do you?"
Valerian:
Even Socrates mocked shortly before his demise, that the man who would carry him away would be ignorant of the fact, that he himself had already escaped a long time before. You told me yourself, that the spirit is immortal, because it emanates from you."
God:
"It is my spirit, my breath that is present within you as long as you live. With your last breath your soul leaves your body."
Valerian:
"Dear God, for me that means that the world of souls is inaccessible for me as long as I live. Then death is quite a radical transition."
God:
"Nobody can avoid death. Death is unpredictable and unfathomable."
Valerian:
"You speak as if death were a person, deciding herself when to come to me."
God:
"I am the Lord of death. By death the soul moves into eternity. The soul is relieved of living through various periods of time and will live in the contemporaneity of all the time periods of

its own former life and also within the universe. The soul lives in its unlimited open strength that can only be quenched within this extensive horizon."
Valerian:
"I think I would like to imitate Socrates. He looked forward to his death. Because in the afterlife he would meat the judges, poets and heroes of old and ancient times and he desired to speak with them. Probably I will meet the one who dreamed me."
God:
"Your perfection may come in death, but not because of death. The end is never tantamount to perception. Death is detrimental."
Valerian:
"I saw many pictures about death, but they were only pictures. But I have this desire for final and enduring fulfilment. I want to be free, not subjected to my will, on par with the angels, without pain, without sorrow about my own shortcomings."
God:
"Valerian, do you contemplate real ddath, or a profound sleep?"
Valerian:
"It will be a long permanent sleep, it will be a dream, a dream in which I live in full, where I will enjoy to see you. I will be redeemed from a reality, where I do not belong."
God:
"Valerian, my friend, you are alive and we are talking to each other."
Valerian:
"You are right again."
God:
"You wanted to use your free will for good things."
Valerian:
"I cannot stop my thoughts and my will.
I see something and I want to have it. I strive very hard to get it. And at this moment I do not ask if there is any sense in it for me or which damage this will cause others."

God:
"You cannot stop a bird to fly over your head. But you can hinder it to build its nest in your hair."
Valerian:
"What strange comparisons you contrive. No nest will be built in my hair. The birds are flying over me, for I have no head."
God:
"The beat of the bird's wings will touch you like a thought that disappears if you do not hold on to it."
Valerian:
"Should I keep holding on to it?"
God:
"I will give you the strength, if the thought is positive."
Valerian:
"These are only promises."
God:
"It is reality. You can rely on it."
Valerian:
"Then touch my soul, touch my spirit. Show me that you are my creator, who gives me strength by his love."
God:
"Who are you?"
Valerian:
"I am a mortal. I am Valerian. But why do you ask? You do know me."
God:
"Look up then. I AM God. I did call you by name. I chose you as a friend and I do love you. That makes you a wonderful person. You are important to Me."
Valerian:
"I am not a talented speaker and my tongue is untrained."
God:
"Who has made man's mouth? Or who makes the mute, thedeaf, the seeing, or the blind? Have not I the Lord? Now therefore, go, and I will be with your mouth and teach you what you shall say" (2.Mose.4:11-12).

CHAPTER VI

Thoughts about Succession

Look into the bottom of your heart
For in there is the source of good
The source can come to live again
If you dig deep enough.

All the teachings Valerian had heard could not make him feel content. He understood that all life had a soul. That everything that is, that was and that will be is a manifestation of the Eternal. Aloud he memorized the words to imprint them in memory: 'Each soul is an indivisible part of the universal soul of creation. Everything in the universe has awareness, no matter on what level it manifests. There is no dead matter and there is no blind unconscious order. Nothing in this world is coincidence. Everything follows the law of cause and effect. The name universe means order. That means that everything existing follows a divine creational plan.
This plan is valid for all spiritual rules.
It is a necessity that such a plan exists, for it regulates cohabitation and living together. One single incident out of plan could seriously disturb the order of the universe and the interaction of its forces. Valerian could feel that some thoughts ailed him and he started to talk to himself and to God: 'I left the old temple out of my free will. I have been made without willing it and sent into a human existence.
To become a human I have learned to think like a human being, now is the time to end the experiment. You told me that life is a game that was made for my pleasure. I did not know this and I can not discern any game.
I do understand now that body, mind and feeling are my instruments of perception, the tools for my actions. I am the one who has to learn the use of these tools.

I am he who knows deep in his consciousness: this part of me, my real being, is not identical with my body, not with my thinking and feeling, not even with my life. You explained to me, that the purpose of life is to find the real purpose therein, and that this will be the only discovery I can make. For this is the key to find the full purpose of my existence as a human being. When I recognize my real self then I will have found you, my God. Then I have
reached the destination of my quest, my centre point.
Then I can be sure that my serious monologue is really a discourse with you. Then I will not need my small self, my ego any more. It was necessary to concentrate my life and my thoughts around an individual centre. The self was only the bearer of the consciousness living inside me.
The period of the ego will end. I did learn that according to my true being I should be immortal and perfect.
Whenever I find a new puzzle stone for my picture I move a step nearer to my goal. This will go on until I can find my true self on all levels.
My basic error was to believe that I exist. As long as this error existed I was a seeker. I had wishes. But their being fulfilled did not quench my desires. Really everything is quite simple. In autumn the leaf detaches itself all alone from the tree, snow is falling, spring arrives, the grass is growing. All happens quite easily, without fear, without a need to hold on!'

"Dear God," he remarked in the end. "The truth is simple. Truth is neither good nor bad. Everything is at it is, if I agree or not. If I do not agree, I will suffer. But if I accept willingly, I might have found the secret of happiness."
This time he received an unexpected answer.
God spoke:
"Ah, my friend, I called upon you to act wisely. Now I counsel you: make your ego your friend. It could become your best friend. For the ego was a good teacher, he led you into temptation several times to force you to make a clear decision. Thus it helped you to get where you are now.
If your ego is your friend it can help you to make the last step.

The step up to your self, so that you can live on as the person you are. Invite your ego to a spiritual discussion among friends. Tell him that changes will not mean his end. Help him to find his true nature, as an individualized part of the one consciousness. Help him to become aware that he is a part of God, who appears in the form of many.

He wanted to take part in the game of life. It was his aim to experience the full entirety of himself. As soon as your ego has lost his fear, when he recognized his true divine nature, you will have a true friend. He will assist you to make the last steps, into your own self, in the unity of all that exists, and to live as the one who you really are to be aware of me, your God in yourself and in everything around you.

Whenever you enter into a relationship with another human being you will have the opportunity to recognize yourself in him and to love him. Everyone you meet is an aspect of God and therefore a part of yourself, will be yourself. Whenever you love, you will love God, you will worship the glory of life in everything that is.

And your life will be full of joy, for you will live in the reality of truth. I think this knowledge can only make you happy. And now listen, what the wise one, Tchu-Ii said:"

'Tchu -Ii the artist
Drew with a flawless hand
Circles more perfect than would the dividers.
Out of nothing his fingers created
Perfection and beauty on the white paper.
When he worked relaxed and quite easy
He never thought of what he was doing.
No effort was needed, his spirit was
Simple and obstacles he never encountered.
When the shoe fits who thinks of the foot.
When the belt fits, who feels his body.
When the heart is in harmony,
there are no pros and cons.
No compulsion, no pressure,
no want and no temptation.

All life is secure.
You are a free man.
Relax and you will do it right, do it right and
You will be relaxed.
Stay relaxed and do the right thing.
The true way to become relaxed is
To forget the right way and to forget as well
That what makes you relaxed.'

(Chinese Wisdom)

Valerian seeks the Logic

In spite of this beautiful example Valerian could not feel relaxed. The question about the meaning of life had him enthralled. Again he was lost in thought. Then an idea brushed his mind gently like the wing of a bird.

Not the things resting in the deep are significant, but those that the future will reveal. Was it prudent to wait here and now for the best to happen?

Valerian remembered the words: *'In order to know me, your God, you have to know yourself. In order to know yourself you have to know God,* I do regret that I cannot see you. It is easier for me to see the picture when I can hear you saying:

'Every day is a present from me given to you, use it carefully.'

'How should I know that it is you who is talking to me? How does this work with seeing and becoming aware of you?' He felt as if caught in a jungle, entangled in clinging vines. Moving forward became more difficult the harder he tried. He could not see ahead and did not know what to expect after he would break through.

'Well,' he told himself, 'if I were God, then all the interconnections would not be a secret for me. But now I am someone who does not know the meaning or the aim of his existence. I only know that this secret is hidden in the hand of

God.'

Valerian wanted to be straightforward and relaxed in order to look at all that happened with dutiful reverence and to find and detect the planning and acting of God therein. He took nothing for granted.

He searched for knowledge that could be applied for useful and practical action, and he tried to find out if also his thinking could be put to practical use, as if he would not only dream a great dream but also set it into motion.

This was the way he was made. Can a dream be truth?

He remembered someone saying: Where there are many truths, there is no truth at all. He pondered this and asked himself:

'Does this mean the same as the word?' All of a sudden he recalled the scriptures of John: *'In the beginning was the Word, and the Word was with God. He was in the beginning with God. All things are made through him, and without him nothing was made'* (John.1:2-3).

In the word there was life. Out of oneness variety emanated. Valerian tried to understand the true life, given by God, tried to understand his self. There was this commandment:

'You shall love the Lord, your God, with all your heart. And you shall love your neighbour as yourself' (Math.22- 37-38).

For Valerian this meant that he was not alone, that there was not only God as a partner in his monologue, but there had to be other mortals, a next one for an open dialogue.

'Someone is living besides me,' he told himself. 'It is possible that two similar beings speak with each other. The spirit of God is living in every being. I am not the exception, I am not a singularity. Only god is not similar to anyone or anything and nobody is similar to him or equals him. Everything is derived from God. In God there is to fault, no flaw, no taint. He is immaculate and unblemished. All parts issue from the entirety and the entirety remains whole, perfect and unchanged.

He is the creator and he is worshipped in the whole universe. In everything is the hand of the almighty. He who is the first and the last one, can be seen and felt.

Boundless and without limits is His knowledge, an endless sea of wisdom. Valerian breathed deeply, he felt nearer to the truth and continued his musing.

'If I speak with God or with other mortals, every talk needs a reason. There should be a question that seeks an answer for the why? The how? Or who are you?'

Plato stated:

'Thinking is the dialogue the soul holds with itself, on the matter it investigates.'

Augustine said that *'even when no words are spoken, everybody who thinks is speaking in his heart.'* In his *'Ideas on the History of Man.'*

Herder wrote: *'As little as man is derived from himself by his natural birth, just as little he is self born in the use of his spiritual forces.'* Humans are capable to bear witness of God, the Creator.

Until now Valerian was convinced that in thinking he experienced a dialogue with God and enlarged his knowledge. That way he had started. Now he had to experience that he had not been made for himself. He wanted to share his experience with someone, wanted to wait for answers, find new questions out of the answers and enlarge the network of communication, Finally he told himself: 'If I had stayed alone, I would not have needed this consciousness.

To think is an act of consciousness. This means for me becoming conscious of something that moves thinking into action. Spirit encounters matter. When matter becomes spirit the full circle is completed. Then attraction enters the field once more. Did I not think some time ago: 'A feeling being, that has a force of will ... and an attractive body, will I be something like that in some time, both in one? If my will wants to create, then will is a necessity.'

Distressed by his ongoing search he asked, as he used to before: »My God, who is this other one, whom I should love as myself?«

God:

»*You have to live in harmony: 'As I am with you, you should be with me.'*

This has nothing to do with my existence or nonexistence. If you refrain from harming others, because you fear to be punished for your acts, or if you do the right things, because you expect to be rewarded for it, you are guided by instable causes. There is no more reasonable cause in this matter then our mutual harmony.«

Valerian:
»As we live this game between us is made in perfect symmetry. When we postulate you our God, we also postulate the continuation of the game outside of this world. The principle is important. But the ethics of earthly life are quite independent from the ethics of the transcendental. That means that the earthly ethics have no sanctions outside time, no final validity. Further on this means that if I commit sin I will be a villain forever.

He who does the right thing is always one of the just.

When I am willing to serve you, oh God, and therefore accept the arguments for your existence, then I have no additional gain in this earthly life. It is only a personal matter.«

God:
»*This principle is based on the precondition that I do exist. If I were not, I could not exist a little bit only, and because I Am, I Am the existing Almighty.«*

Valerian:
»Being the Almighty you could not only create another world, but could also make a different logic instead of this one that is the foundation of these deliberations.

Within such a different logic the hypothesis of temporal ethics would be invariably linked to the transcendent ethics.

Then logical evidence, if not the apparent evidence would come into force and the hypotheses could be accepted: God can be manipulated by threatening to commit sin against all reason.«

God:
»*An Almighty God is also an all knowing God.
Omnipotence is not independent from omniscience.«*

Valerian:

»So to speak, one who is omnipotent, but does not know what consequences the acts of his almightiness could have, is in fact not omnipotent at all.«

God:

»Quite right. If I performed miracles, as they report, that would shed a doubtful light on my perspective, since a miracle, as a sudden intervention is an interference with the self autonomy of creation. If I adjust a project of my creation to perfection, whose course I know from start to end, it will not be necessary to interfere with this autonomy.«

Valerian:

»With your ongoing omniscience, if you interfered in spite of this, it would mean that you would not improve your creation in the least, since improvement means that there was no omniscience at the start, but that you show your existence by performing miracles. This is a breach of logic. Could I say that when you set such signs you want to give the impression as if you nevertheless wanted to repair creation's logical imperfection. My logical analysis is: Everything created, including us mortals, would be subject to improvements that do not come from ourselves, but are coming from you, oh God. But then the miracle should be the standard, so that humans are so much perfected that no more miracles are necessary.« [7]

God:

»You seem to develop. However, miracles, the occasional interventions could be more than simple signs of my existence. Besides the fact that they give proof of their creator they confront the recipient with the question, did the miracle serve to help someone down here? The logical relation would be, either the created one, the mortal is perfect and independent then no miracles are required.

But if the created ones are not perfectly autonomous, then miracles are necessary. Wonderful or not wonderful, I can

---

[7] *Extracts from Stanislaw Lem "The total Void"*

only improve what was imperfect. One could say in other words, to signal my presence by means of miracles is the application of the logically worst method, to manifest My Presence.«

Valerian:

»Please, my God could you reveal to me if you wished that there would be an alternative between logic and the faith in you?

Maybe the act of faith means to renounce all logic in order to have absolute trust in you?«

God:

»Presume that I am acting this way because I want to be attainable for the mortals. In one word I request the rule of faith above logic. This is quite possible. At a certain point you have to leave thinking and contemplate presumption and raise it above logical certainty. This is done in the name of unlimited trust. This may create logical discrepancy, but also an additional value, the faithful call it 'the Secret of God'.«

Valerian:

»The disadvantage is that this Secret is based on infinity.«

God:

»Then think about it.«

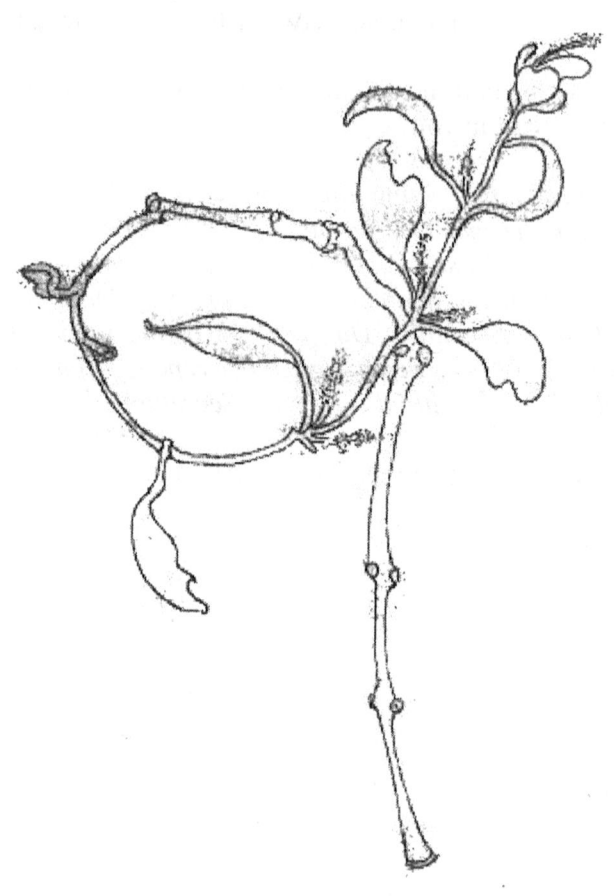

CHAPTER VII

Include Love into your Deliberations

The glowing message of love took hold of Valerian. The words *'love your neighbour and love your enemies'* affected him deeply. It seemed to be a simple formula for the coexistence of humans but he could not imagine its practical application.
Valerian hesitated, tried to overcome his scruples, before he dared to ask the next question, finally he spoke his thoughts aloud: "Almighty God, I believe since it pleased you to make this world you also want that humans adapt the world for themselves, as they can or want it to be. We have to assume that they want to live on this world. But the coexistence of many creatures implies a lot of difficulties.
I doubt that all of them could live because of good and constructive words. That would mean that they all strive towards the ideal of love notwithstanding serious resistance."
God: *"This is the most difficult task of all. I remind you of the words of St. Paul 'Do not let yourself be defeated by evil,*
but vanquish evil by goodness' (Rom 12:21). *When Christianity emerged, it was clear from the start that it was a principally new ethic, unknown until then, that brought a new understanding of man and his place in the world. The sermon of Christ on the mountain renounced the ancient ethics and launched the new concept of love. New commandments are not always derived from more ancient ones. The new idea here was the negation of the old rules, their suspension. You must have heard that before your life began the valid principle of action was 'eye for eye, tooth for tooth'. The new teachings say: 'Do not fight against evil, but if someone hits you on the right cheek, then present the left one as well.*
If someone quarrels with you to take your tunic, then give him your coat as well…… what you want that people should do to

you, this way you should act for them,' wrote Luke." (6:29-32)
Valerian:
"The people in ancient times, as I would call that period, lived in hardship, fighting against nature and other humans to get a place in the sun and to earn their bred.
They had to hunt for all the amenities of life. No one got anything for free. In this fight for existence, be it legal or illegal, the strong ones were victorious. That means that they applied not only their wits but also their whole being in this fight."
God:
"In reality people became haughty and proud. They adored a culture of force and violence. This pride and this violence were the obstacle and because of these the faith in creative love could not prosper. Remind yourself that also in your own life it will not be easy to understand what I demand, 'do not fight with evil'."
Valerian:
"That is right, I do not understand it. How can you demand any such thing? Should I relinquish dominance to evil? This is an absurdity from the point of view of my thinking, since you did explain to me, in which way I can use my free will."
God:
"Kindly remember that formal logic and the common sense of philistines are afraid of the absurd, while life, culture and art can handle the illogical and the absurd, the wonder and the paradox quite well. Mind the words of Tertullian ... 'credo quia absurdum' - they are not only a demonstrative challenge to barren everyday thinking but also the imperturbable foundation of faith, the most important principle of being of mankind."
Valerian repeated again and again:
"Do not fight against evil! What a strange demand!"
God:
"This is not meant to be a call for passivity and laziness. It means that you should not fight evil with physical force, because with this kind of resistance you will enhance evil and

diminish goodness. In my attitude of mind evil has no personality of its own. It is nothing but the absence or diminishment of goodness."

Valerian:

"Do you want to say," he asked sceptically," that when I fight evil with its own weapons, so to speak with evil, that I will diminish goodness?"

God:

"Yes, you could phrase it this way. The only effective way to fight evil is to overcome it by doing the good and right things. If you foster goodness, so that it can prosper, evil will go away by itself, because only goodness will be left. The most active and effective force in this fight is love.

Listen to what I tell you: It will be the task of your life to help that the force of love will make a breakthrough within all of mankind."

Valerian did show his indignation and answered: "You set me a practically unsolvable task. Sorry. But I simply cannot make it."

God:

"Well you can, otherwise I would not ask it of you. I give you this task.

You will spread the ideal of my all embracing, ever present and all forgiving love. The life of your ancestors was ruled by fear. Yes, all humans feared Me.

Then I sent my Son to them. He spoke to them of My love.

This did not eliminate their fear, but its importance was diminished. All his teachings, his life on earth, his passion, his ignominious death on the cross in expiation for all sins of mankind, all this should be seen as an act of My overflowing abundant love for humanity.

St. John wrote later about that love: 'God did not send his Son into this world to judge the world, but that the world should be saved by him' (John. 3,16-17).

This unimaginable love for mankind made Paul deduct that in reality nobody would give his life for another.

'Now hope does not disappoint, because the love of God has

been poured out in our hearts by the Holy Spirit who was given to us' (Rom. 5,5). *Love is vigorous and forceful, love surpasses all knowledge."*

Valerian:
"You are speaking of the Holy Spirit?"
God:
"He is the principle of Change."
Valerian:
"The principle that changes man ?"
God:
"The Spirit emanating from Me that can change human thinking and human feelings, the Spirit that creates the manifold diversity of reality. As you know My Spirit does not rest immobile in itself, He is movement and continuous course. We discussed this earlier."
Valerian:
"The spirit is also within me?"
God:
"You will become aware of Him, you will feel his influence in the moment you believe and when you start with your task to convey to mankind the example of My infinite love."
Valerian:
"What shall I do? Why do you set me a task that is beyond my strength?"
God:
"You are a follower. You are loved by Me. From you I demand only one thing, you will be handing out this love.
Remember, what has been written: Jesus said to him: "You shall love the Lord, your God, with all your heart, with all your soul, and with all your mind.
This is the first and great commandment. And the second is like it: 'You shall love your neighbour as yourself.' On these two commandments hang all the law and the Prophets' (Math.22:37-40)."
Valerian:
"You should love your neighbour. Here is another riddle for me."

God:
"I will try to solve it in a simple way. If you tell Me that you love Me, this will be untrustworthy for Me, when you do not comply with the second commandment. For if someone says, 'I love God,' and hates his brother, he is a liar; for he, who does not love his brother whom he has seen, how can he love God, whom he has not seen? (1.John. 4:20). *The love for your neighbour is the necessary precondition for the love of God. This is the most important step on your way to Me. Therefore be attentive. He who loves his neighbour fulfils the laws. Love will not harm another human."*

Valerian:
"This kind of love surpasses the possibilities of mortal men."

God:
"I do not set tasks or give demands that can not be fulfilled. With each new task I will give you more strength and self-confidence. You will grow with each task. I do cherish human thinking and human feeling and I never give contradictory demands. Kindly remember, love was known to your ancestors, the philosophers of antiquity, and they divided it up in two different forms.
One was the sensual desire, called the common Aphrodite, and the divine Eros, the celestial Aphrodite, as a cosmic force.
But basically the y did not know a thing about the all forgiving love of your next one, the love that alone can make humans more similar to God."

Valerian kept silence and thought. 'Be similar to God' …. 'Become similar to God' … would he really want that? But how ? 'Be like a god? I do not think that I could ever achieve that.
And I remember that once I presumed that if I can not see you, then you can also not see me.
Thus quite unconsciously I made myself up to your image.'
Finally he sighed aloud and said:
"In consciousness I will never succeed with that. It is quite impossible for me."

God:
"You have to eliminate the word 'impossible' from your vocabulary. When you are challenged, do not ask if it is possible, for every challenge seems impossible at first. Rest assured I will not lead you to tasks which you could carry out easily. My conceptions are just humanly impossible.
This is a necessity because otherwise I could have not part in it, as everything is possible for me. Try to start correctly, if the beginning is in order then also the ending will be correct."
Valerian:
"If I start correctly, then I will also end correctly. If I do not start in the right way, then I can not end the right way."
God:
"What I request is trust."
Valerian:
"I do know" that. Would you also give me the courage to proceed on this way to become one of your heroes."
God:
"A hero of faith, my hero of love, of hope, meaning you will be a man with positive feelings. I need you for this work, this work needs you. I can not do it without you."
Valerian:
"You want me to help you. That is great honour indeed."
God:
"I do have a plan for your life. I did call you by your name."
Valerian kept silent and thought within his heart:
'Will I become o hero? Can that be possible with the help of god? All this is surely just a dream.
How did I get involved in all this?' He tried to get rid of the idea that God would need him, Valerian, that God could love him, Valerian. Then suddenly he heard God speaking to him:
"My dear friend, after all the ancient philosophers St. Paul also wrote about Christian love.
"True love,' he said, 'is accompanied by the joy and the perfect union with the beloved one, the complete coming together in the act of love, the profound knowing of each other, that does not happen on the level of reason but in the

other, inner core of personalities. This knowledge is not a simply human one, but divine, for 'he who loves God will be granted knowledge by him' (1.Cor.8.3). *This empirical recognition is not founded on reason, and comprises not only 'human matters' but extends as well to 'divine matters'. For the love that exists within one human being, is for him the crown of virtue and understanding, of temperance and patience, of fear of God and brotherly love.*

A human with these gifts he will be neither lazy nor barren. This way love is as well an important Gnostic factor. Without love there is no higher super reasonable cognition, which I recommend to all my followers, for without this recognition nobody can achieve neither salvation nor everlasting bliss."

Valerian:

"Do you mean to say, that all good intent, all the good deeds of humans, all knowledge, talents that you granted them, that even faith itself in your existence, that they all are invalid without love."

God:

"Yes. Love is the ultimate blessing, love is the most precious gift. Without love all the good deeds in the world make no sense. Love is the culmination of the ethical and essential completion of man, the link to perfection. Listen, I will honour you with the same task of which St. John spoke to his followers: 'Beloved, let us love one another, for love is of God; and everyone who loves is born in God and knows God. He who does not love, does not know God, for God is love' (1.John 4:7-8)."

Valerian:

"These words of yours do they state the essence of being a human?"

God:

"These words reveal my love for mankind. For St. John writes further: '..... in this is love, not that we loved God, but that He loved us, and sent His Son to be the propitiation for our sins....Beloved, if God so loved us, we also ought to love one another' (1.John.7:10,11). *Yes. I Am love.*

Unfortunately the majority of people do not understand this. Some very few, who grasped this highest ideal of human life are often considered to be either crazy or ill."

Valerian:
"You want me to speak to mankind of your all embracing love, the love that is your holy identity, the love that is blessed by your authority."

God:
"Yes, because I do love you and all of mankind.
And with all my might I wish that all humans should love each other unconditionally. Unconditionally means: 'If you love only those who love you as well, what sort of gratitude will you gain?
The same applies if you do good only to those who are doing good tings for you, what sort of gratitude would you earn? You have also to love your foes and try to do good without expecting something in return, then your reward will we great.'
This reward will be: '..... they shall have my own self. If people love each other, then I remain with them and my love is completely within them' (Luk. 6-33-34).

Valerian:
"The one who loves you unconditionally and understands you. This way, he will be your equal, he will be free and independent and will be free from fear before the mighty of this world and even before you.
Will everything be possible for him then?"

God:
"Yes. Love as the supreme form of existence takes away the fear of God."

Valerian:
"What a thought. You will make me one of your followers. You do give me high credit. What will happen if I disappoint you?"

God:
"You are a thinking and feeling being and every intelligent being needs motivation. I should mention that I am highly interested."

Valerian:
"For me that means that I should be interested in the topic of our discussion, because otherwise there would be no discussion."
God:
"Just so. I would have no inclination to talk to someone if I were not motivated by interest. Interest is simply a constellation of unconscious propensities.
When I speak to
someone all these inclinations are brought together. This is the result of an immense amount of small preferences, propensities and inclinations."
Valerian:
"Interesting. This is a very human way of thinking. Humans possess something, something within them, something, well I mean, they have some sort of inner fire, something animated, that flares, fluctuates, wavers, but this something is creative. I do know this because of my origin."
God:
"Wonderful. You are drawing a pretty picture of the soul."
Valerian:
"The picture of the flame makes me think of candles, of fire, of thunderstorms with lightning flashing across the sky in embarrassing patterns."
God:
"You do understand that you are talking about the soul? Out of flickering lights they form scintillating patterns.
The soul is like a flame and I am lighting this flame. The soul pours out the glittering rain of love. Already the early German mystics used the metaphor of fire when speaking of the soul. Master Eckehart preached my ideas: 'The divine seed within the human soul glows and glistens, shines and burns and streams incessantly upwards towards God'."
Valerian:
"This is a very strange thought. So the stars are not the home of the souls. What a game of words. A flame cannot think, a flame cannot feel!"

God:
"Could I convince you that a flame has its own force, a force that is not physical?"
Valerian:
"A force one has to be afraid of?"
God:
"When you are within love, then you will have no fear. Love is a force that also gives warmth. All parts of the universe are conserved by warmth. The soul with its conscious and unconscious forces is an objective reality, a reality that supersedes the single person and determines his reality, rather than that the person himself determines reality. The realm of the soul is more vast than that what you could experience as your inner life. The spark of fire, as you depicted it, is the symbol of the individuality of the soul."
Valerian:
"A long time ago Heraklit said: 'Fire is gifted with reason'."
God:
"The stoic school of philosophy took up the teachings of Heraklit. Zenon spoke of fire as 'an artificially acting principle that creates all things on earth. Truth is that fire permeates all beings. The eternal moves in every thing, and every thing is an image, a symbol."
Valerian:
"That reminds me of a thought that was already brought up by Goethe. He said that the flame was a symbol of God. Now I ask you, a symbol of what?"
God:
"In the Name of the One, Who created His Self."
Valerian quite shaken:
"You are God, you are CAUSA SUI?"
God:
"You have got it. I Am the Cause of My Being. I Am the 'Eternal Light' that came into this world. He who follows Me will not walk in darkness, but he will have the light of life" (John. 8:12).
Valerian:

"You rob me of all speech. But my thoughts do not give me a pause for consideration. But I remember what Goethe said about the flame of fire, that it was not a God, but a fitting image of God. In the Bible fire plays an eminent role where your appearance is concerned. You appeared before Moses in the burning thornbush (Ex. 3,1-6).
From there on our earth is considered holy, since you ordered Moses: 'Take off your shoes, for the place where you stand is holy ground' (Ex.3,5). I am convinced that does not only concern the place where his feet were standing."
God:
"You are right again."
Valerian:
"The Holy Spirit also appeared in the form of tongues of fire. Did you not tell me that you would send me the Holy Spirit, if I decided to become your follower. Oh God, sometimes you make me quite desperate! I am afraid there is no sense in resisting you. At the same time it gives me strength. Maybe I will find some humans who carry a small flame within themselves without knowing it."
God:
"Maybe. Remember the flame as a symbol of the nature of the human soul."

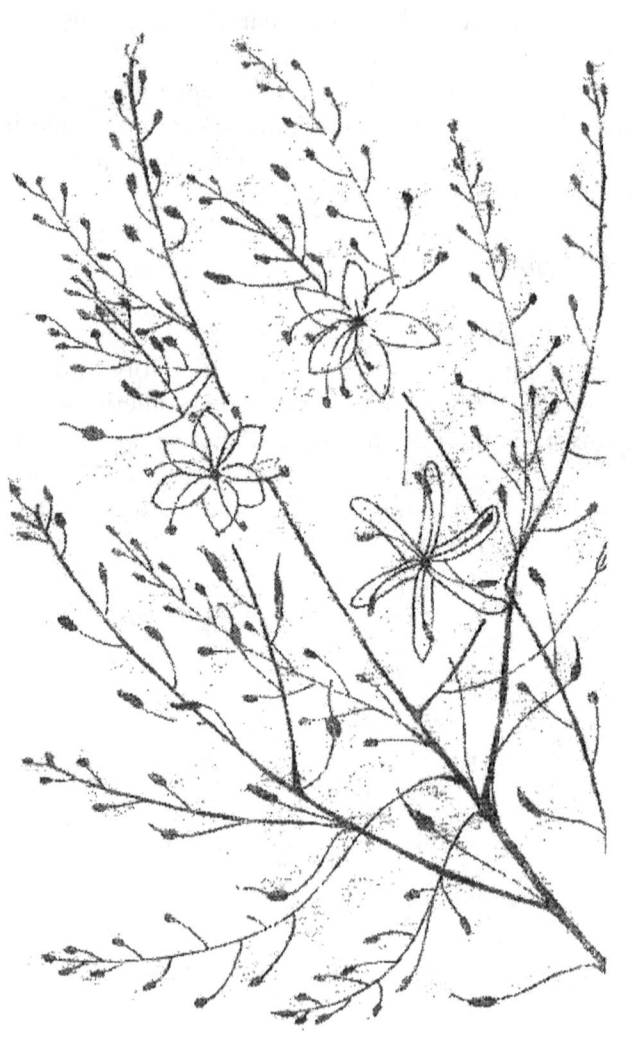

The Question of Justice

Valerian declared instantly:
"Well, you spoke wonderful words. But you remind me of the Roman aristocracy, for them human life was nothing holy. Duty, honour and fame were far more important than any human life."
God:
"In order to stimulate your imagination I will tell you that I brought about some changes. According to the directions set by the stoic philosophers new laws developed. These laws would serve to enhance the freedom and dignity, the individual diversity and originality of the human personality.
The roman writer Tertullian attacked his fellow citizens severely because of their inhuman cruelty, that showed in some of their customs and their public games, where human blood was spilled abundantly.
The others retorted that only the blood of the gladiators, fighting against wild animals, was spilled[8].
Therefore the new laws should be valid for all humans and protect their lives. Then I had to act Myself: I gave all My love to mankind. I gave them my own Son to save them all from their sins, the Holy One for the unholy, the innocent for the sinners, the just one for the unjust, the immortal
One for the mortals. Out of love for mankind I made this world and everything on earth is given to them. I formed them after My Image and gave them a mind. So why do you not want to take up the task I gave you?"
Valerian hesitatingly:
"To be your follower, or as you say to be a hero for you in faith, or to try to imitate you, is a tremendous task."

---

[8] Dr. sc. Victor Bytschkow 'Love as the foundation of human existence.'

God:

"It is. But this does not mean that you should dominate your fellow humans, that you should use force against the weak ones, or that you should strive for wealth.
If you want to follow Me, this will only be possible if you take up the burden of your neighbour, if you do good deeds and
give your goods to the poor. Then you will be an image of God. I call upon you to become My follower in love for mankind."

Valerian:

"This love will be my effective weapon against violence and evil?"

God:

"You spoke truth. What you need is love for all humans and true humaneness. They are the most important attributes of the human mind, if the mind is wise. Christianity tried very hard to distance itself from its heathen ancestors. But they also concealed that several good ideas were brought up by the stoic philosophers. Thus they never spoke of Seneca or Epictet."

Valerian:

"Seneca as well as Heraklit declared the soul to be a spark from the substance of the stars. Plato on the other hand taught, that the souls had been created only after the fiery stars and that each soul had a corresponding star for itself."

God with infinite patience:

"I do know all of this. May I counsel you not to avoid them and kindly try to show the late antique philosophers the devotion that is their due. Without any prejudice you will find that the apologists developed the idea of humanitarianism with great consequence and practical applicability, they made it the centre of their ideological system.
Certified with the authority of God they tried to apply it in everyday life."

Valerian:

"You gave wisdom to man. Therefore for the ones who dedicated themselves to wisdom, the recognition and the worship of the true God take precedence above all."

God:
"Some people confuse wisdom and scholarly knowledge.
The wisdom that emanates form me, creates the variety of active life.
The same wisdom flows continually through all created varieties and binds them together into a coherent unity.
Wisdom is more fluent that any movement, wisdom permeates everything" (Wisdom 7,24).
Valerian:
"Kindly permit me to come back to the thesis of Seneca, who described wisdom as the perfect gift of the human soul. He called it the knowledge of the divine and the human or in other words: 'Wisdom is the knowledge of the divine and the human and all its causes' (44.2).
God:
"This addendum seems quite unnecessary to me. For the causes of the divine and the human, they are only a part of the divine. But philosophy has decreed either one way or another. Some said, it was the propensity of virtue, others spoke of the urge to better the heart, and some called it the striving for real knowledge. You can be certain that there is a difference between philosophy and wisdom, for it is impossible that the object of an aspiration, and the one who strives for it, could mean the same. So it is with wisdom and the love for wisdom, for the first is success and reward, or wisdom will come, and the love of wisdom attracts you to it" (89, 4-7).
Valerian:
"How do I use wisdom?"
God:
"You should be wise. Wisdom is the condition of perfect thinking; to be wise means the use of the perfect thinking" (117,12.16).
Valerian:
"Did ever some man achieve to live such a perfect life?"
God:
"There were many who tried, for them the worship and the knowledge of the true God were of the utmost importance,

followed by humanitarianism, mercy, compassion and love for all human beings. This is the area of ethical principles, the foundation of a new culture. The noblest link that unites mankind is humaneness. This link should not be severed. Because then the right to be called 'a human' would be extinguished."

Valerian:

"I do understand. What requirements are needed to keep up humaneness?"

God:

"Just to love all human beings, because all humans are of equal value. Nothing is more contradictory to human nature than discord. I have to give Cicero his due, when he said that a human who lives according to his nature, can not harm another human being. If it is not according to his nature to harm another fellow human, then the vital feature of human nature is to help each other."

Valerian:

"How is it possible that the wise ones of ancient times were not moved by compassion?"

God:

"What an absurd idea. Do not dwell on contradictions and half ruths. Try to ask a wise man, what he recommends when he sees that a man is threatened by fire, when someone is drowning or is trapped injured beneath the ruins of his house? In all this cases the judgement will be that humaneness decrees to rush to the aid of the afflicted. If reality was then as you suspected, how can you think that they did not want to assist those who were suffering form thirst or hunger, or froze in winter without proper clothing? There is no difference. The long centuries of suffering, the tears and the indignity of the greater part of humanity, which brought on the crisis of the ancient world, made man realize that without compassion and mercy he could not survive, but would be reduced to animal state or perish."

Valerian:

"The picture becomes clear. One has to follow the truth and not its shadow.

Nobody can help all those who are in need. But when I do not help a person whose life is in danger, then I will be guilty of his death. Is that so?"
God:
"You did mean the right thing. But do not talk about guilt.
If you want to talk about guilt, then you should have an inbuilt sense of justice, you would like to play the judge about human behaviour. Beware, do not judge others, even when you think that they violated the commands of human mercy.
Remember the words that Matthew wrote: 'Judge not, that you be not judged; For with what judgement you judge, you will be judged, and with the measure you use, it will be measured back to you' (Matth. 7:1-2)."
Valerian:
"Oh Lord! What a confusion of ideas. Of course one has to agree that guilt is a terrifying term. Someone could become guilty simply because of an inconsiderate action.
It is difficult not to give an immediate judgement, if one is concerned about justice, because justice is certainly a virtue."
God:
"To be concerned about justice and to stand up for justice is a virtue which may quickly lead to setting up demands."
Valerian:
"What kind of demands?"
God:
"Quite a lot of humans want to exert their own ideas about justice in small personal things and as well in a large political context by means of force. I do not know any human who could say about himself that he was one of the righteous. The important step is to recognize one's own shortcomings and weaknesses."
Valerian:
"Probably it is not easy to find out one's own shortcomings. If it was easy everybody would do it."
God:
"Only a few are capable of this. But in order to 'confess' your own weaknesses you have to 'recognize' them first.

What you criticize in others mostly stems from the recognition of your own faults.
Many people just love their own weaknesses and hate them at the same time."

Valerian:
"And you know it all and you see it all?"

God:
"Yes."

Valerian:
"The words I spoke earlier, well I tried to describe an example of how to act in a fair and righteous way. I thought that it would be right to give to everyone what is due to him, and treat equal things equally. Essentially I will give my attention to the other one: *'est ad alterum.'* In this sense Plato said *'that the essence of justice is that everybody does what is his due.*[9]*'* The roman law expert Ulpian declares *'that justice is the ongoing effort to grant every person his right'."*

God:
"All humans have different points of view. The demand that every person does his due makes only sense, when you consider that by nature not all humans are the same, that they all are highly different. The unjust one disturbs the basis of the community. He makes common action and cooperation impossible. In his interpretation Plato refers to the state and the graduated construction of society at his time, so as 'to give everyone only what is due to him, and not in equal measure for all', and in this way to make it possible for everyone to reach the level of perfection, that was attainable by his nature, avoiding that his life became frenzied or tormented.
The demands made upon each person were determined by the natural potential of this person.
Plato adhered to the idea that man could come as near to the divine as his own nature permitted."

---

[9] Commentaries from Plato Essays on the State, 'The Flame of the Hearth.'

Valerian:
"He did write: *'A beautiful soul will make a beautiful body'* in 'Phaidros'. Probably for him beauty was the visible expression of the spiritual and the divine. The ideal divine gestalt was quite corporeal for him.
A God, in the sense of the *'divine entities'* was for him an immortal being, with a soul and a body, both linked together for eternity."

God:
"Quite a special idea, you should think about it in depth. So I tell you the real goal is and that is the important thing to keep the soul pure and thus beautiful. The path to this goal is given to every human. Many people loose their way, some are searching for it as long as they live. We did already discuss this. There is not much to add to this: Every creature and every instrument has a destination of its own. Varying opinions about justice do not lead to cognition. The important thing is the essence of justice, if you want to form an opinion about the luck of the righteous and the misery of the unjust. You mentioned 'guilt'.
Guilt is the same as sin. Sin in itself is the contrary of love it does not serve the beatification of the soul. In sin man turns against his fellow men and against a community with God."

Valerian:
"If I do not help, I become guilty I said earlier. Maybe this was not correctly formulated. Besides if such a situation occurs, I would surely help the unfortunate or do whatever is possible for me."

God:
"I presume you would. With my help you could also achieve the impossible. You should always act with consideration. In regard of sin I must say that it offends me, because if offends humanity, because some person will be hurt or suffer injustice. Sin is the negation of love.
This means that in committing an offence against another human being, this person does not only infringe the other one's rights, he also says NO to God.

He who does injustice to another human being injures the self esteem of this person. In order to overcome guilt it is not enough to exchange the 'evil willing' against 'good will'.[10] *If a human being turned his back to God it is not enough that he repents his misdeeds. He needs the forgiveness of God, so that the communion between God and human can be re-established.*
For the community between human beings and God is founded not only on the good will of the human being but essentially on the will and the grace of God."

Valerian:
"A carelessly spoken word can lead to complicated new questions. But essentially the striving for a just balance could not be bad?"

God:
"Yes, but again this is a new vast area. I tell you, he who caused damage to the rights of a fellow man shall repair the damage. If this is impossible, for instance in the case of a murder, then the perpetrator should do penance in a way that equals the gravity of his crime.
Penalty can be a means of reconciliation when the culprit accepts it. It is not important if penance is decreed by an earthly or a heavenly judge, the important thing is that the wrongdoer is willing to demonstrate in a credible way his intention to improve by doing good works in compensation."

Valerian:
"Finally I get a new opinion on this topic. I am really grateful that you drew my attention to this. Gradually I become adept in listening to you and in understanding what I hear.
With the help of your strength my insight expands. I wish for the well feeling that prudence can give. Maybe you will lend me of your strength?"

---

[10] Extracts from 'Basic Command Love', by Hans Rotter, Chap. Love and society.

God:
"Prudence is not a feeling but a virtue. Prudence is the life force of the senses, the soul and the spirit woven together. If you ask me nicely I will help you to develop the great virtues of courage, prudence and understanding."
Valerian:
"I presume that in order to be just all these virtues are essential. But to achieve them all I will need more than just good will."
God:
"Yes, but kindly leave it to me to point our their weaknesses to my people. I do know them all. I am a very forgiving God. Remember the words my Son spoke on the cross: 'Father, forgive them, because they do not know what they are doing' (Luk.23:34). Well, I forgave them."
Valerian:
"Then, Oh Lord, only faith and trust is left for me."
God:
"Do I not know that your mind cannot cope with all this. When Christendom was young and lived under the dominion of the Romans who judged by cold reason only, it was difficult to explain to them, why sick and wretched humans should be kept alive. Humanity is a deep feeling, the soul's very own property. In ancient times as well as today people ask for my help in critical and difficult situations.

I am not idle. I induce people to act for the good. It happened quite often that rich heathens distributed their wealth among the poor and many became Christians. Some developed a passionate eagerness to achieve socially equal standing for all people.

Augustine proved that the idea of love led to a new sight of the world. And Paul wrote the significant lines: 'If I had all wisdom and all secrets and knowledge were mine, and if I had all the faith, so that I could move mountains, but if I have no love I am nothing.

And if I distribute all my goods to feed the poor, but do not have love, then it will avail me nothing. Love does never end.

There remain faith, hope and love, these three. The greatest of these three is love' (1.Cor.13:2-3: 13).

Valerian:

"My Lord this means that I should strive for love, because it leads to the knowledge of God. I hope that I can understand now."

God:

"Indeed, my dear, I tell you this: Love is not an end in itself, but it connects you with me. My love is stronger that the natural tie between a father and his child."

Valerian:

"I begin to understand. ….And I should follow this,… this…" He took a deep breath, could not end the sentence he had begun and kept silent until God spoke to him again: *"Do not be afraid. Whatever you will be doing among people, your actions should be filled with compassion and true love. When you acknowledge this it will be easy to love your neighbour like you love yourself. Because it fulfils the desire of your soul."*

He does even distasteful chores
And he loves me
With all his heart.
Why does he not change into being you?

(Hank Cochran)

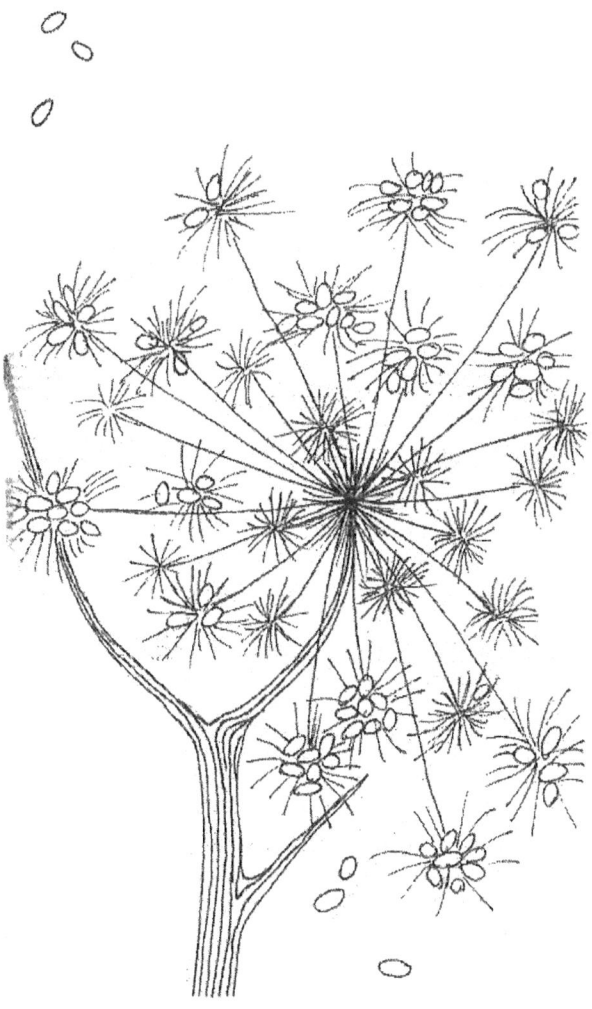

CHAPTER VIII

The Question of Consciousness

Deep in his thoughts Valerian continued on his way along the stony path.
The multitude of ideas moved him but was no encumbrance, the flood of ideas streamed through him towards an outlet.
He was still searching for the knowledge, the real knowledge, the singular one. He felt that he missed practical experience, the living example, he was surrounded by pictures and symbols and he understood that he had to encounter other humans. Again he started to talk to himself: 'I can doubt that I as a mortal do exist. I can doubt that I see and hear and feel and think.
The me, who sees and hears and so forth, can therefore not be identical with Valerian and his head. But if I doubt that he exists, I also doubt that I exist myself.
But I am here. I have hands, they are holding this stone.
How do I know that they are *my* hands? How do I know that this is *my* body? It is controlled by me. Is it then mine? In a certain sense yes it is. Since it is mine, I can use it as I like, as long as I do not harm someone else. In a way this body is a sort of legally granted property.
Even if I can not sell it rightfully during my lifetime, I can give over the property of my dead body to a medical institution.
Although I do have this body, I am something quite different than this body. When I tell myself my body is
mine, I do not mean that this body belongs to me, probably quite a useless statement.
Or does anything that belongs to nobody belong only to itself? Does the moon belong to everybody, to nobody or only itself? What and who can be the proprietor of something? Well I can be one, and my body is one of the things that belong to me.
Anyway I and my body they seem to be both the same, tightly

connected but differing at the same time. I control my body, mostly it is under my control. Now I ask myself could I, when that is so, exchange my body against another one, a stronger, more beautiful and more obedient body? How would it be if my brain was transplanted into another body which it could control then? Could that be an exchange of bodies? Well there would be technical problems. I am convinced that in case my brains were transplanted into another body, I myself would also be transplanted. Or am I my brains?

I do have a brain that functions. Now I got to know that what I am is not only a living body that has a soul, but because of that soul also a spiritual being. And this spiritual being belongs to God who made it. This is the birth place of my own history.

I do have a life of my own. I do have consciousness. But what in this world is consciousness? Do other living beings have a consciousness? Do they have the same one as I do? Should I be conscious of the fact that I do have consciousness?

Can anyone have unconscious thoughts, unconscious pains or feelings or perceptions? Am I conscious when I am dreaming?

The things that I am conscious of and the way of my perception of them, decide *how* it is to be myself.

What would it be like to be my own reflection in the mirror? Nobody else can know as well as I do what it is like to be myself.

How does that fit together with the searching presence of someone, that is the Divine Spirit?'

'The realities seem to float in a far reaching sea of possibilities, wherefrom they were selected somewhere, say the indeterminists, all these possibilities exist and they are a part of the truth.'

William James

Valerian was agitated and restless, then he felt the challenge to follow the Lord.

He got exited about the thought that he should meet other humans and would talk to them about the positive ideas of

God. But at the moment no human beings existed around him and therefore he complained: "Oh my God, I cannot fulfil your command. For a person, that does not exist for me, cannot get help from me, nor can I injure him. If you, the God, the Creator thanks to your omniscience, does know from the start that all creatures will be grateful to you and will love you, or would be ungrateful and rebuff you, then you will cause enforcement. Enforcement is not understandable with my present perception."
God:
"This is why so many intellectual and logically thinking people have declared that nothing is due to God: neither love nor hatred, neither fear nor punishment, neither gratefulness nor reproach, neither hope nor reward, nothing is due to him."
Valerian is distraught.
"That is mere conjecture. I mean that without a consciousness these problems would not exist. Without consciousness a lot of feelings would be less interesting and less complicated, or we would not even experience them. In my opinion consciousness concerns only feelings, for consciousness it is unimportant if I touch a stone or not."
God:
"My dear, your interpretations are quite interesting. I would like to explain that humans have so many problems in their life because of their lack of love. You have to trust Me. I do know you and I know all life. I gave My love to all human beings. For them I made this world. But given love can only speculate why it is returned. That is understandable."
Valerian:
"Love that relies on speculation in regard of the existence of the beloved is nonsensical. He who is almighty can grant surety. If he does not give surety he deems it unnecessary."
God:
"Unnecessary for whom?"
Valerian:
"Unnecessary for mortals. Excuse me please, but I just assumed that you might not be almighty after all. A not almighty one really merits feelings that resemble love and

Gratefulness, but no known to me theology will permit this. So to speak we serve only ourselves and nobody else."

God:

"Every human being is created first of all for himself. Everyone has his special personal value, so that he is able to serve others or let others serve him. Every person lives his own life, but he does not live for himself alone and he does not die just for himself. He or she lives and dies for others. A human being lives so that also others will live. Real live is only possible in a community. If man had been created a singular person he would not even have a name. Nobody would have given him a name, nobody would call him by his name. He would not know what it is to be a human, he would not know anything about Me, the Creator-God. So he could not talk about Me. He would be a nothing, a nonentity. Every human being lives only conditionally with others, but unconditionally for other human beings. Nobody can exist alone permanently. That is the meaning of creation. At the beginning We Made not man but a pair, a man and a woman."

Valerian:

"Well we are to serve each other and that is all."

God:

"Quite so."

Valerian:

"I was made as a thinking being."

God:

"That is what you say about yourself."

Valerian:

"I do not ask for privileges."

God:

"Why should you? Did I not tell you that only love for each other gives people viability, that love for each other gives them the ability to get away from humiliation and hatred and befriend each other. Love is not there to raise oneself above others."

Valerian:

"Did you not say that you love mankind?"

God:

"That is right. To be in love means simply 'to be in God'. Where people work for one another in love there I work together with them.
This was meant at the beginning with being in the image of God and thus it will be accomplished in the end. When you start to do good I will help you to accomplish it. You will have to take decisions. You alone decide if you will be happy or not. I grant you the choice.
But I counsel you: free your thoughts from sorrow, just live, do not expect much and give a lot. It is important to know that destiny can not be larger than you are, it cannot exert any power on you."

Valerian:

"Being a mortal I am at the mercy of destiny, whose reigns I cannot hold, but I have to endure what destiny has decreed for me? I cannot finish my way by my own strength."

God:

"Just learn to adapt. That is wonderful enough."

Valerian:

"I believe that I still have difficulties to answer the question if I will be able to love others."

God:

"I presumed that you command your thinking, but the way you talk it appears to be the other way round.
I did already tell you and I repeat it now, so that you will learn to understand: 'Your live has been given to others and will be taken again from others. When you meet another human being, always remember that in him or her you will meet Me, and you will meet yourself in the other one.
The freely given affirmation of faith and love in god can be a symbol for the approval of your fellow men. Only if you do approve of yourself you will be capable to love your fellow men and only if you can love other humans you can love yourself. If you take up love and rejoice in it, you will get to know the value of your own personality. If you do not want to acknowledge this, then you will have to consider the love given to you as not justified and will have to rebuke it.

This will lead to self-contempt and even selfhatred.
The capability to accept your own personality would be highly restricted."

'The capability to accept my own self,' Valerian repeated this to engrave it in his memory.

He sat down on a rock and remained quietly there to put his thoughts in order.

Slowly he sensed the change that worked within, he felt that his intuitive will was getting stronger, while his physical will diminished. He felt a similarity to the snake he had wanted to catch earlier, who had avoided his touch by relinquishing its old skin.

Again he fell to brooding. 'Who am I? What can I do? I am a mortal, I live here at this riverside, here among the temple ruins, a temple built a long time ago for the gods, that was then destroyed by some enemies, put to the torch and consumed by the fire. What can I do?

Why did the destruction occur? God taught me that it is just and good to be against violence, and to give peace and wish for tolerance.

I have a relationship towards God. He is as He is, unchangeable. When He speaks of love, why does HE have enemies?'

"Oh God," he stammered in a very human way. "Do we have common enemies?"

God:

"What do you mean?"

Valerian:

"You said that you loved humans. But many humans do not love you. They bear you enmity. This could also happen to me, when I happen to love a human being."

God:

"Humans are not my enemies, even when they oppose Me. They hate only the image that they themselves have made of Me. This difference must be considered. We did already talk about this. To declare their enmity towards Me in reality, they would have to stand before Me and see Me as I Am.

You Valerian, you have an enemy. He is the evil. Evil takes up different forms. Evil comes as violence, greed, murder.

Evil appears in the guise of a friend. But evil is not the true enemy."
Valerian:
"The total of evil is not the real enemy?"
God:
"No. Evil is the symbol of the enemy, it is the result. The real problem lies in the heart of the people. It is the problem of soul and spirituality. They have a flaw. They do not have inner peace, so they hand on their own destructiveness."
Valerian:
"Do you mean that they do not love themselves?"
God:
"If they were capable of love they would not destroy, but would build bridges."
Valerian:
"Maybe they do not have faith?"
God:
"This could be it. They lack he faith that the fire of my love burns within their hearts."
Valerian:
"If they knew it, they would feel that you are alive within them, then they could begin to be the men and women as you wanted them to be."
God:
"Maybe, if their aim is righteousness. There is no guarantee for constancy."

What will you do in this world?
It has already been made.
The Lord of Creation considered it all,
Your lot has been cast,
Persist in your strive,
The path has begun,
Complete now your journey,
For sorrow and grief will not make a change,
They lead you astray from destiny's way.

Seng Ts'an

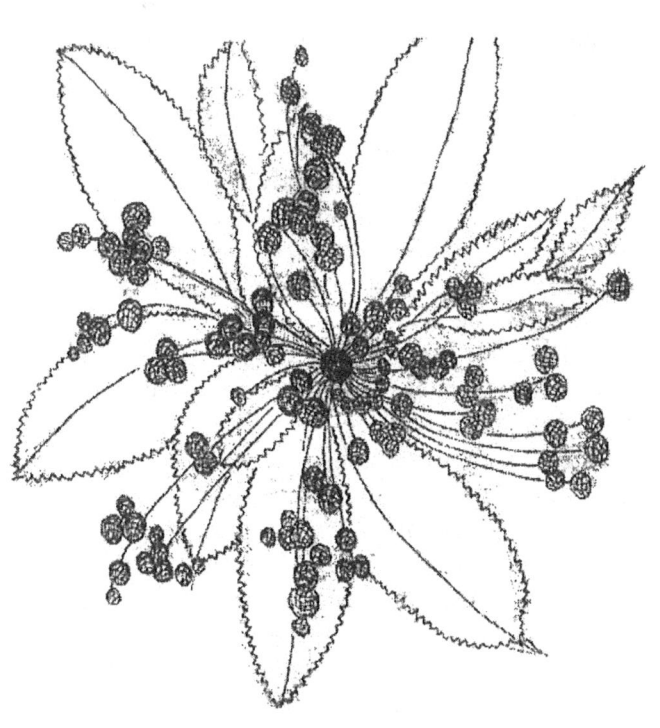

Valerian looks into the genes

The beginning was simple. It is difficult to understand how even a simple universe commenced. 'I think that it is even more difficult to explain the complex formation of a fully developed order of things, of life or of the being that could create life. Then there are the things around me that I see and they should be explained as well. Each single raindrop lasts only a moment.
Rocks and the waves of the sea can be large or small.
Natural selection in its commonest form just means the differing survival of structures. Some live on, some die. If this selective death should have some influence on the world, an additional condition has to be fulfilled. Long proven processes of automatic selection continue in their blind and inevitable way as they did in all the years past.
Genes do not have foresight. They do not plan. Genes just exist and some exist stronger than other ones. That is all.
But the properties that determine their longevity and fertility are not as simple as they were before.
A gene will have quite a lot of consequences for different parts of a body. A body part is influenced by a multitude of genes. The effect of every single gene depends on the mutual influence of many others. Some genes function like managers, they control the activities of entire groups of other genes. Compared to a picture each page of plans contains indications on the various different parts of the structure 'man' and each page makes sense only when the references to other pages are duly considered.
The history of reproduction leads to a mixture and regrouping of genes. This means that every single body is only a transitional vessel for a short-lived combination of genes. The genes themselves are quite long–lived. In the course of generations their paths are crossing all the time and in constantly new configurations.
A gene can be considered a unity that survives a multitude of individual bodies following one after the other.

The genes are the immortal ones or simply stated: the genetic unities converge on immortality.

We as simple mortal beings can expect to live some dozen decades more. The lifetime of the genes should not be counted in decades but in millennia.

Assuredly a living being is more than the sum of his parts. The imagination of my own body feeling will help me here.[11]

Another question arises: Is the soul more that the sum of its parts? When I am standing before a mirror and the light is extinguished then the image will vanish.

What is this, this ME?

'When I take out one stone of the puzzle that I made some time ago, then the whole picture will be ruined. If I do not find the proper puzzle parts or put them in the wrong place, I will never make a harmonious picture.

All parts are related to each other.

Applying this idea to my life, then corrections are necessary if mistakes have been made, and more deliberation and prudence are required in order to avoid mistakes. I do have a free will. It has been formed in a long ongoing process.

When the wind rustles the leaves of the trees, the leaves are moving. Are they doing this because they want to move? Or are they just being moved? I can imagine a mechanical hand and have it make the same strange movements repeatedly. Would it not be an unbelievable coincidence if the imaginary hand always tried to grasp the same leaves? Probably not. Still more unbelievable if these movements of the hand were always the same, stable ones, never damaging one single leaf. It can be presumed that the branches are hanging down tightly together, and that chance happens as well on a higher plane.

---

[11] Extracts from 'The selfish' by Richard Dawkins

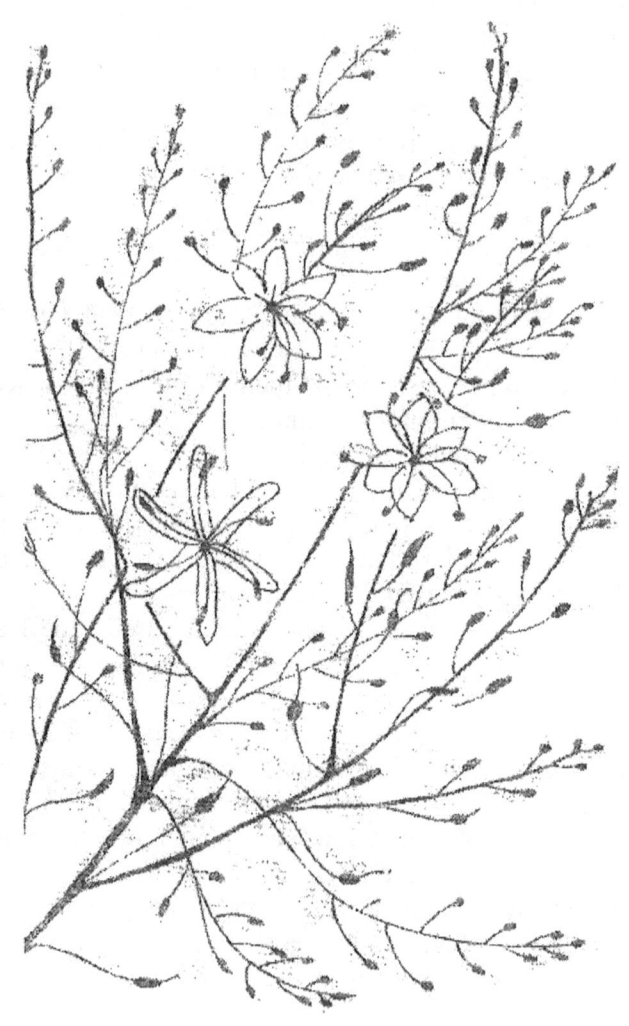

The brain needs this structure consisting of multiple layers, because it has to cope with an unpredictable, dynamical world. Rigid structures are doomed to die out.

But what is this, this ME?

Valerian mused 'when I am dreaming, am I then conscious? Do others know if they are conscious or not?

The contents of our consciousness is what experts call all those events that are accessible by inner experience. The nerve cells produce awareness.

Awareness is at work when the brain has to do important things, if it has to be kinetic, sensorial or cognitive and more.

No recipes exist, no programs, no modules. The entire brain is involved with the development of awareness.

Now with this knowledge, my initial question what awareness means, becomes an unsolvable mystery,'

Valerian stated for himself and lead his thoughts back to those experts who claimed that our awareness is removed from the grip of natural sciences, but that awareness consists of two substances that are indivisible.

'Maybe awareness functions like a lamp that can give light or remain dark? If it was similar to light, then it would exist always it could never be not.

Is it not written: *'You are the light of the world. A town that stands on top of a mountain cannot be hidden. You do not light a lamp and hide it under a bushel, but set it in a holder and the lamp will give light to all that are in this house'* (Matth.5: 14.15).

Conscious experience is a vastly spread phenomenon, like the light that cannot be perceived by the eye, the light of whom Jesus said: *"I am the light of this world, he who follows me will not wander in the dark"* (John. 8:12).

Valerian continued on this way of thought and considered: 'The two mentioned substances the personal awareness and self consciousness are something different.

Without doubt awareness does exist in countless forms, all of them inconceivable for me, or they exist on other planets, in other solar systems, everywhere in the universe.

However varied the forms may be, the fact that an organism can have conscious awareness is wonderful.

Personal experiences form the cornerstone of my power of imagination. Together with mental processes they are the cause of my behaviour.

I am bound to the contents of my own mind, and this mind is limited.' Valerian confessed to himself and he continued his thoughts. 'However it will be impossible for me to think that I could become similar to God and I exclude to become a wanted follower; although to imagine a likeness or placing myself in this position is quite tempting. But this can lead me astray. And as I cannot manage this task, I declare, that I can not take up this chore. There are certain facts that a mortal being can never comprehend.'

When he finished his contemplations he called out to God again and asked another question.

Out of the jungle of his thinking he cried out: "Great God, how do I discern self consciousness from self awareness, how do they both function, and how can I discern them? Answer this one question and I will stop to bother you."

God:

"My friend, a long time ago we spoke about your will and that you have a physical will and also a will of the soul. I tried to explain to you that your physical ego will decide about your physical will, it would permit or not. You declared at the start of our conversation that freedom of will meant ethical responsibility and that this ethical responsibility would be too heavy a burden for you."

Valerian:

"I do remember. But I also said: the freedom of will gives me the capability for sin. And I do not want to commit sin…"

God:

"If you do not want to commit sin, why then do you do it, I ask you?"

Valerian:

"Yes, My Lord, I have become more prudent. You did instruct me. But there is this new problem."

God:
"To make you understand, I will give you an example. Let us presume that you want to become rich and that you will succeed in this.
Let us further presume that now you wanted to acquire this land where you now stand as your own property. It should belong to nobody else but you."

Valerian:
"This sounds enticing. But it is only an example and you did choose it. Now if I did agree, what will happen when the land belongs to me, when it is my sole property?"

God:
"This question of yours tells me that you will not be content in acquiring the soil alone.
If you were satisfied in buying the land you would have no more questions. It would be yours and that would be it."

Valerian:
"That is the decisive point. I ask you, what shall I do with this land? But you already know the answer."

God:
"It was my intention to connect something else with this example. Now you confirm that my assumption was correct.
The ownership of land is not the end of your wish but only the start, to build a new temple on this land, you could find artists and give them order to make new sculptures to your liking, to have this tiger here repaired and so forth."

Valerian:
"I would not be content for my wishes and my creative imagination would be encouraged. Did you want to stress that fact?"

God:
"I would presume that your riches would prove to be a burden for you. Nobody was made really happy with money. Quite the contrary, it brought with it an ever growing greed. Before thee many have lived who wanted to have more than everything. Shortly, what I wanted to make clear to you is quite simple.
You know your body, you are quite sure that this is your own body. Your brain is part of this physical substance.

By the work of your brain you are able to will what you want.
You might want to be rich and use all possible physical means to this end.
You could tend your body and love it. But there are functions within your body that are not subject to your will.
A simple example is your heartbeat, your breathing. All your glands that produce the necessary ferments to keep up your bodily life, they have their ordained place and their order. That way you are a human being.
And consider, even with the strongest of wills you will not be capable to walk on your hands for a long while, to change into a being where the feet would replace the hands, or where your head and face would be turned backwards.
You can turn around a straight and vertical pole but you cannot
transplant your heart into another location within your body.
Even if you could do it and this would bring about a lot of problems, with all your will you could not change the beat of your heart, speed it up or slow it down."

Valerian:

"That is quite right I can follow you here, but..." God slightly irritated: *"Kindly wait with your interruptions, your mind is flexible, it is willing to accept these ideas, that there is something else... for instance that you have no head. You are quite ready to accept the idea that there are things that are as they should be; and that there are other things where this is not the case, for instance like being a ball or being a moon."*

Valerian:

"And what is the sign of true knowledge?"

God:

"Already your forbears tried to explain with different formulas what it is to be a feeling being. They spoke that there must be an 'inner life', of 'making experiences', to have 'a point of view', or 'to be ones own self' or 'to have a free will'.
They all tackled the emotional basic question if it made sense to immerse oneself into some object or not. Is there something, they asked themselves, to which this desire is related? How would it be to be an illusion? How would it be if I were you?"

Valerian:
"That is not possible. I do not even want to think of it."
God:
"Take up the idea, that there is a soul in your body. A soul like a flame that can light up or die down, or like a candle, where the flame moves on from one candle to another, from body into another."
Valerian:
"You link that to the question how it will be if I extinguish the light of a candle and then relight it again?
Will it then be the 'same' flame? Or even when it stays lit is it just from one moment to the next the 'same' flame?
As an example the Olympic flame is carefully tended, when every fourth year it is carried by sportsmen across thousands of miles from Greece to its new destination.
The idea is of utmost importance, that this is the 'same' flame as the one lit in Hellas. Even the shortest disruption in the transfer chain would destroy the symbolic value of the flame if people got to know about it, whereas if they were not informed the symbolic value would remain.
Why in the world should that be important at all? But emotionally this plays a major role. So this image of the 'flame of the soul' cannot be easily extinguished."
God:
"What an interesting explanation."
Valerian:
"To be here and now is an imminent experience for me."
God:
"For your personality this is a central experience. You cannot determine 'here and now' without having it related to your person. Just like 'now' and 'me' are 'here' and 'me' tightly interwoven attitudes of the mind."
Valerian:
"Knowledge is a strange phenomenon. Knowledge can be transferred and jointly owned. I would like to experience, that the same words will also have the same meaning for different persons. Can two people really speak the same language?

What I mean when talking of 'the same language' is a delicate thing. We presume as a given fact that the secret meanings are not common property. We know what we want to hand on and what not. But each word is surrounded by its own spirit, by a cluster of ideas, and we know that try as we might to bring them all to the surface, something will always be amiss, more than an approximation is not possible.

When I take all this together, it is not as easy as assumed before, to be a person, me, now in this moment. Just as I cannot see how you are seeing this person of mine."

God:

"You are a vessel of the spirit. The spirit is the wanderer, who on his way through the land of men, commands the human soul to follow him, the spirit, to his true spiritual destination."

Valerian:

"We already talked about this. But let us return to my question. You tried to explain to me the will, the aspirations of the person, the physical man, but what about the other will, the desire of the human soul?

You did say that the soul has a will, a will that would be stronger than the will of the mind. What has this to do with the intention to buy this piece of land?"

God:

"I did not forget it. But know at first, that self-assurance differs from self awareness, but both are indivisible. The same applies to your physical will and the will of your soul.

Let us assume that I am the Creator-God, the Spirit since the dawn of history, the total entity, the one self, the one being. Out of this CAUSA SUI all life has come into existence."

Valerian:

"What has existed before? Was there something?"

God:

"That makes the same sense as if you would ask what was there before birth? I Am God. I Am the origin and the force and I was before creation. Out of Me everything has been made. Everything in the world consists of the same primordial material, by My creational force countless beings were made from it.

My SELF is independent from the multitude of names that people gave Me during their long lives. I Am the ENTIRETY. 'I Am Who I Am', as I instructed Moses (2.Mos.3:14)..

I am not something put together out of different parts. I remain the inscrutable entirety, from where creation comes to pass and is ongoing and disintegration is impossible. I give but do not receive. Out of Me from my being flows the divine seed, the never ending stream, the creator spirit into every living creature, so that every being participates, every being is a part of Myself.

A part becomes several parts, parts become particles, they split, they multiply, they become a network and are interwoven into a universal net. The weaving goes on.

Every living being is a part of the whole and within the entirety. A small self is made out of the vast entirety, this Self is a being that creates. The created human being is therefore similar to God, but never the same.

By your nature you share something of the divine. A part of My Mighty Spirit lives within you. Therefore you are a part of My own Self, you have a share of This Self. That makes you a person.

The spiritual link enables us to speak to each other. You could talk to yourself in the quiet calmness or speak to Me without words. If you would not have a spark of the Divine Spirit, you would just be a lump of flesh. You cannot be divided into a body and a spirit. Bodily and spiritual qualities are intertwined.

Every single human being does not live alone but is linked to the entirety. Therefore no human will cease to ask for completeness, even if there is no final answer. Humans strive to find the boundaries of knowledge, to get down to the basic causes. It is a mistake to want more than the entirety.

The human body and its physical functions, engendered by primordial fathers and mothers, developing through genetics, will continue to exist. As long as humans procreate in a healthy way, they will remain a biological part of nature.

All human bodies are linked in a way by means of their genes. But their live is not just a part of biology. They all are woven into the universal net of the world by invisible threads.
The earth is visible, but you can understand it only with the help of the Divine Spirit within man.
Only by My Eternal Spirit the invisible can be understood."

Valerian:
"When people speak of brotherly love, as they do in Christendom, this cannot mean relationship because of ties of the blood. If, as you say, all humans have the same origin, there should exist a spiritual bond that links them together."

God:
"Finally you show some understanding. All creatures have the same creator. However everyone is an individual personality formed of flesh and spirit. Thus existence does also set a task. You have to discover the self that is alive within you. You have to get to know your own self and respect this self. This means that you have to become aware of yourself. In the end this self assurance will lead you to the knowledge that God is alive within you, because you are a part of this greater Self. This recognition will make you respect and value life.
This awe of life is also the key to love. Inasmuch as you value yourself, you will value your neighbour and will not do him any harm. Only this way will you come to understand what makes a personality. The human person is a creature made as an image of God, therefore humans do have creational force themselves."

Valerian:
"This reminds me of a poem that was written by Goethe some time ago:

‚Man reluctantly only gives reverence and awe,
And mostly decides to deny them forever.
Some higher mind was granted
To the nature of man.
But only the most favoured ones
Developed these gifts by themselves,
From time immemorial

*We worship these great ones
And honour the Saints'."*

God:

*"The basic principle of awe is mostly misunderstood. It has nothing to do with fear, but implies respect before life. The spiritual bond between humans binds them together in the feeling of pain, sorrow and joy, and that love can be lived.
Every single being, but also the entire world, are each of them a single distinctive entity."*

Valerian:

"Do you want to say that no living being is just a singularity, but can mean a plurality?"

God:

"Just so, that makes the difference. For I am both: the creator of plurality and the force of unity. This is the basic construction of all reality. Were I not the force that binds everything together, there would be only isolated singularities, but not a world of beings, forming a harmonious universe, even when they contest each other."

Valerian:

"A long time ago the philosopher Hegel wrote about unity within plurality. Since all single beings, and the whole world are manifold and diversified parts, the construction of the universe and its tiniest components reflect the nature of their creator, divided and yet as one. Therefore the entire universe is am image of God Himself. Could it be that self-knowledge and selfassurance do stem from there?"

God:

*"The capability to love yourself is not related to your body, even if your body would be of perfect beauty, but is related to this knowledge of yours, that God is present within you.
You will be aware of my Self within you."*

Valerian:

"I do understand. Then I could not act 'unselfish', if I am convinced to do good for others, for that would mean to act without any connection to God. I could act mercifully and unselfishly if I acted according to your intentions."

God:
"You got that right. I feel we do understand each other again. You can love your neighbour without regard for your own person. For if you want to do something good, you will not act selfishly, only for your own benefit, but for the benefit of your neighbour. You will feel compassion.
You will feel with the destitute. You want to give away something of your own to alleviate the plight.
I would not call this an unselfish act, but rather an altruistic one. Unselfish implies that you do not consider your own self. Since compassion comes out of your inner self and not from your Ego, compassion comes from your soul and not from your physical will, you will act not unselfishly but be altruistic.
This is the difference. I do not split hairs. Naturally you can relinquish something, 'let go' of a thing. You can drop something to the ground or place it somewhere else.
It is quite something different to let go of yourself, to come free from your own control. You can devote yourself to another human being and with the help of the other person find back to your own self. You cannot relinquish yourself as a person. Your ego is bound to your self. This is my link to your soul, to your spirit."

Valerian:
"Did I get that right, in my self, that is a part of your Self, of the entirety, your spirit is alive within me. Then my Ego, my physical body is your home, your house. Or should I say my self resides within my Ego? Should I be aware of this?"

God: *"Right again. There is a link to my creational force, you and all humans are My creatures, gifted with your own creational strength and capable of extraordinary things, you can cope with the demands of everyday life and achieve the impossible with my help. You are capable of positive feeling, of joy, love, faith and hope.*
When you can find the truth, when you can perceive Me in yourself, then you will know happiness, harmony and contentment.

Such a life will radiate and sustain like a far reaching light. If you want you can compare this to the bearer of the torch with the Olympic flame."
Valerian:
"Maybe I had this in mind somehow. But what will happen when the light is extinguished, when I die?"
God:
"Your self is not final, as the body is. I gave it to you as long as your life lasts. Then it will return to Me."

CHAPTER IX

What is the desire of my Soul?

Valerian was still standing on that piece of soil, where he had stood for a long time. Suddenly he felt something beneath his feet, something that flt as if the earth moved beneath him. A movement as if the continental shelves had shifted to trigger an earthquake.
They moved in one direction and not back. He made one step away from the spot where he had stood, looked to the ground and was sure that he had been moved. He lost all sense of time. He looked around and admired the brilliant flowers, blooming all along the hillside, as if he saw their riches the first time. Flowers and flowery bushes of all colours and sizes filled the air with their sweet fragrance, bees hummed and crickets chirped. The leaves of the huge tree rustled and birds sang their airs.
He leaned against the trunk of the tree and looked about him astonished and quite changed. He stretched out his arms with the palms of his hands extended towards heaven as if he wanted to beg: 'Please give me all that I could not see and feel until this moment.' And he closed his eyes before the brilliance of the sun. 'I am one of those,' he said to himself, 'one of those whom God loves. I am one of those for whom God is incomprehensible, and I cannot understand even myself.
But am I also one of those who are willing to live according to His will? I want to be free from fear. I do not want to be violent. I want to live in peace. But how will I accomplish all this with my will?
"Great almighty God", he claimed asking for help.
"Will it be in accordance with your will that lives in my soul, that I should see this life, my existence, in such perfect beauty?"

God:
"Yes, because the willing of your soul is the flowing transmission of my will. If you want to do something and perceive that it will increase your love, then you will know that your will and mine are in harmony. For I will all that is good and pure, I want harmony and peace. In order to find this within yourself you have to be good."

Valerian:
"That is not much."

God:
"You have to follow my commandments."

Valerian:
"That will not be difficult if you will help me, if you will guide my will with your own."

God:
"Do not think that this will be easy. As if I should help you to carry your provisions up that mountain there, and then partake of your repast on the mountain. To keep my commandments will require all your strength. This will require all your faith and all your love. Did I not tell you 'I do not exist, just a little bit.'

Entirety demands everything, not just 'a little bit'.

Listen, entirety gives all, not just 'a bit', it gives the whole life, not just a little bit of life, the entire personality, not just a bit of a man, the entire soul and not just a bit of a soul, the entire creation, not just a bit of the creation, or just a bit of the universe, a bit of the stars.

Therefore my first commandment is: "You shall love the Lord, your God, with all your heart, with all your soul and with all your mind. This is the first and great commandment. And the second is like it: 'You shall love your neighbour as yourself'. This you can read in the book of Mathew (22-37-39). You have every cause to know that you have a self value, this is the reason that makes your love of yourself grow. Remember forever and everywhere: none of My commandments should be observed 'just a bit'."

Valerian:
"This surpasses my possibilities. Probably I will not be strong enough."
God:
"My commandments should be understood as spiritual not materialistic."
Valerian:
"Even my spirit is not strong enough.
Remember when I first called out to you I did beg you to take away my free will, because I did not want to fall into sin, yet with only my will ......"
God cut him off in the midst of the sentence.
"Yes, my friend, I do know that. Your problem starts with this way of thinking. If you would love yourself with all your heart, then you will not want to commit sin, for then only the will of your soul will act. Then you will not harm anybody because you would not want someone else to harm you. It is quite simple. Do not have just a bit of feeling, but a total feeling and you will not be just a bit human but a true man!"
Valerian:
"With this weakness I am not alone. Consider what St. Paul wrote ages ago: *,For what I am doing I do not understand.*
For what I will to do, that I do not practice; but what I hate, that I do. If, then, I do what I will not to do, I agree with the law that it is good.
But now, it is no longer I who do it, but sin that dwells in me.
For I know that in me (that is in the flesh) nothing good dwells; for to will is present with me, but how to perform what is good I do not find.
For the good that I will do, I do not do; but the evil I will not do, that I practice.
Now if I do what I will not to do, it is no longer I who do it, but sin that dwells in me.
I find then a law, that evil is present with me, the one who wills to do good.
For I delight in the law of God according to the inward man.

But I see another law in my members, warring against the law of my mind, and bringing me into captivity to the law of sin which is in my members.
O wretched man that I am.
Who will deliver me from this body of death? (Rom.7:15-24)."
God:
"But Paul wrote further on when he acquired more knowledge: 'So then, with the mind I myself serve the law of God, but with the flesh the law of sin' (7:25). Can you not perceive here in a rather wonderful way the two different kinds of will. The will of the spirit, of the soul compared to the will of your ego, your physical body. For the spiritual law of a life in Jesus Christ has freed you from the bonds of sin and death. When St .Paul said: 'For those, who live according to the flesh, set their minds on the things of the flesh, but those who live according to the Spirit, the things of the Spirit' (Rom.8:5). This explains and should be understandable even for you, that my spirit dwells within your soul. Paul was a man as you are a man.
He fought with the will of the soul against his physical desires. The fact that he lived in another time than you do is of no importance at all."
Valerian:
"You have known for quite some time that my problem is to learn to make a distinction. How can I perceive the will of my soul?"
God:
"Well, my friend, do we not talk to each other?"
Valerian:
"That is right, but how can I find my way in any trivial situation?"
God:
"You ask strange questions. Are you a child or are you a man? Rest assured, if you trust me then you will get what you need. You have to believe. All your questions will find their answer. Sometime later you will get knowledge. I am in the streets and squares and I touch life, I heal the sick and care for them in my way.

It is not the importance of your problem, or my love for you and all humans, it is not the depth of your faith, if and when I will answer your questions and hear your cry for help; it is according to my perfect plan when and how I do give an answer. You have to trust my all-embracing plan if my answer is limited or comes too late in your opinion. You have to learn to trust."

Valerian repeated slowly and with a certain self contemplation: "Of course we talk. I ask the questions and then keep silence, then hear your voice and you answer me." He moaned: "Oh God," as all of a sudden, with his eyes closed, his reflection stared at him. He stared with his eyes into the depth of his own eyes and sank deeper and deeper until all bodily senses vanished and he felt only the vast, bright, boundless universe around him. With eyes closed he listened to the beating of his heart."

God:

"My eyes are set on you and my ears are willing to listen to you. Your eyes look at me and your ears can hear my voice.
I cannot be an object for you, for I am the subject.
Therefore also the contrary can be absolute. When someone denies God, he will not harm God, he will destroy himself. If someone defies God, he defies himself."

Valerian opened his eyes and saw the clear unchanged sky above and the luscious flowers around him. He heard the song of the birds and the hum of the bees. "Oh my God, how could I defy you? By your will everything was created. I enjoy the rise and the setting of the sun. I look at the mountains and the sea, I can see the clouds and the rainbow after the storm. I see lighting flare and feel the calm. Nothing of all this I can change with my will. I just accept it and rejoice in it."

Valerian stood, extended his arms and looked again across the rocks and the walls of the ancient temple on to the waterside and felt that something depressed him, something he had lacked the courage to voice until now.

"Well now," he shouted into the silence around him, "if this place where I sit, or go, or stand on, the soil that moved beneath me, this piece of earth, where you did talk to me, if

this land was my own, my property, what would that change?"
God:
"That would not change anything now. You should have listened to the will of your soul earlier. Your soul knows you and would not want you to buy this land. But you did not listen to your inner voice. You wanted to follow your will."
Valerian:
"This is not a bad desire. I did not hear you say that I should not want to do this. You even asked me the question … if I would buy the land, when it was offered to me."
God:
"Quite right, it was my question, a kind of test."
Valerian:
"I do not understand."
God:
"It is my wish to see you contented and full of joy. But your will strove towards discontent. What was offered to you, you considered as paltry. You wanted more and more and you forgot the beginning. For you wanted not only to have the land, but to build a temple on it with gorgeous sculptures. You desired fame, thus you became immoderate."
Valerian:
"What do you mean with moderation?"
God:
"You desired not only to have this wonderful spot for yourself, in memory of the talk we held here. Therefore I asked you: do you want to own a lot or just enough? And now I tell you, he who has a lot will always want more."
Valerian:
"You hold me in a poor regard, do you?"
God:
"I know you. I do promise you that everything will be a lot easier for you if you trust me, or if you will cherish the will of your soul!"
Valerian:
"Did you want to explain to me that I should pay more attention to my inner feeling?"

A Symbol

Valerian proposed:
"Everything would be easier for me if I could see a symbol, something that would influence me in a positive way whenever temptation arises. For a moment he looked across the land before him and declared: "I will make you the active symbol of myself consciousness. You did explain to me that myself being and myself consciousness are in harmony. Then I became aware that a part of you is alive in my person. Since to be aware of something is also the question of one's inner conviction, the representation of this awareness requires for a proper self consciousness a proper symbol. The Symbol of the great SELF, that is available for oneself as an image. Important for the distinctive characteristic of the Self Symbol is not only its appearance, but the significance that the symbol has for me."

God:
"A special idea. Why don't choose a visible and also an invisible Symbol? Why don't choose the cross? We have already discussed the importance of the cross. The wood of the tree is the Symbol of the new order of the saved world: 'ecce lignum crucis, in quo salus mundi pependit'."

Valerian:
"Yes, I remember. We spoke about this when you suggested that I should talk to a tree."

God:
"Quite right. Let us suppose that you choose the cross as your Symbol then you can recognize in it the old and the new era, the human will and the divine will.

It is the sign of the axis of the world and the sign of ever forgiving love, because the Christ is the axis of the world.

I do advise you to take the cross as your Symbol, you will need it. The cross stands for faith, hope and love. It is the Symbol of human guilt and human greatness, and for the thanksgiving for everything that was, that is and that will be.

To put it short: it recalls the past, it represents the present and

points into the future. The cross is the symbol for death and resurrection, for 'die and live anew' as Goethe described it..
You see the cross in everything you come to know. It is the second guiding principle of thermodynamics: entropy."
Valerian:
"How tightly they are linked in one presence: 'ecce homo'. Really I am quite surprised by the calmness with which you address the universal process of decline with the one word: entropy. The sense of our talk is not to speak about molecules, positions, balance, possible accelerations and collisions, about these things that create disorder. Let us leave them to the scientists. One of those was L. Boltzmann. The application of his deliberations in regard of the universe as an entirety, considered to be a closed system, makes cosmological theories appear quite questionable. With ever increasing entropy the world would move towards a final state without energy and difference in temperatures. This would mean the end of all materialistic occurrences. Science calls this the thermal death. And I, the mortal do have this question: Is your world a closed system? Did you decide this end? Is this your will? That makes me sad. I am wroth to contemplate this."
God:
"My friend, the sad fact is that humans are working hard for their own destruction. Their curiosity makes them believe that they can know it all. This is the great error of all the knowing ones and those who should know even better. They see the goal of science in a sort of totality of knowledge. Modern natural science has increased knowledge, but it did not increase wisdom.
People will feel that even when all possible scientific questions have been answered, their problems in life have not been affected in any way.
So I tell you, to believe in a God means to ask the question for the sense of life. To believe in Me, your God, means to see that knowing the facts of this world does not solve anything. To believe means to see that life has a sense.
Returning to our original topic I tell you: not far from this spot,

where you are standing now, you can see the ruined temple and the crumbled sculptures that were once glittering in marvellous colours, proclaiming the glory of their builder. You wanted to acquire this land in order to build a new temple with new sculptures. Let us neglect the fact that this would bring unrest, that the calmness of this wonderful place would be disturbed, I counsel you that you should try to get hold of the time with all its events, because such as it was and as it is this time is irrecoverable.

Secondly you should consider what would heat and wind, fire, water and air do with it in the future? They would let it fall into decay. Soon it would look again as it is now, maybe it would be worse."

Valerian:

"You deprive me of all my energy. Can I live in such a way that it will cease to be a challenge? Then I should live like you within eternity and not be bound to time."

God:

"You have your life. Your life will make the sense that you give it. You have a healthy body. You are conscious of your awareness. You have the capacity to think."

Valerian:

"Maybe the symbol of the cross is not quite the one I had in mind. I want to see the 'living God'."

God:

"I Am the living God. I do reveal my existence in the sphere of wisdom and through the knowledge of chemists, physicists and other scientists. Many scientists learned something about me. Many used their lifetime to develop theories, speculations and ideal structures about this.

But they never in their entire life really knew Me, their God. They neither know my presence nor what I Am, neither do they do not know, what I Am not. If they knew, life would have another form."

Valerian:

"Well, that is your statement. But consider: even I cannot prove your existence or non existence. The best I can do is to draw an intelligent conclusion from the things I do know. No matter can create itself. This is my point of view. I have been made. I did not have any choice in this.

You gave me a brain, a memory that files remembrances that I can recall later, when I need them. Your intervention is needed so that I can continue thinking,

when you ask me to do so."

God:

"My dear friend, as long as you live this life of yours I will be with you. When I told you at the beginning of our conversation that the duration of human life is an inadequate conception of time, did you not reply that you preferred to be taught by pictures, that you would look at an hour-glass. But the hourglass does not depict time only its movement. Besides time is not an object.

The last outreaching horizon, from where all others are enveloped, is without boundaries and endless. For the end of time as well as the beginning of time are both inconceivable for you. You are not able to think about a 'before' or 'thereafter'. The stoic philosophers stated their opinion that a human could find fulfilment in death, just by wanting him to occur- because thus the end would become the fulfilment of a human will - they just forgot to see that someone destroyed in this way cannot experience this fulfilment, because he does not exist any more."

Valerian:

"My Lord, your choice of language is amazing. The moments of quiet tension arising during our discussions, they give me the feeling of life.

I see the beauty of this world when I open my eyes and I can feel that you are near and make me feel well when you talk to me.

You are full of surprises. In the moment where I think to have understood something, you present me another riddle.

Although I know that this situation cannot last forever.

But maybe I can feel now what is essential. It is the profound power of perception of things, even the perception of the cross

as the symbol of love. I can see the cross when I close my eyes and I see you, and I can feel the heartbeat of my life. Your will alone, creator, binds me like a duty."
God:
"It is my will that mortals should help each other."
Valerian:
"You taught me that love means to respect the individual personality of the other person."
God:
"You got that right. Do not forget I am nearer to your inner self that you yourself are. This is also valid for all your fellow humans. Saint Augustine wrote a long time ago: 'intimior intimo meo.' As you can never see yourself completely, you will never find completeness in yourself, complete your knowledge. You have to choose, if you want to act in the light of charity or in the darkness of egotism.
By this you will be judged."
Valerian:
"Yes, but anyhow all things in my life that developed differently to my wishes are an integral part of my reality. I try to read from your words that your doings are part of my life's process. Your will meets with my will, your unlimited love envelopes my mortal existence.
With our mind we cannot comprehend this."
God:
"You see everything too difficult and complicated. Really it is quite simple. Just relax. My counsel is to take to your heart the words of Matthew: 'Do not lay up for yourselves treasures on earth; where moth and rust destroy and where thieves break in and steal; But lay up for yourselves treasures in heaven, where neither moth nor rust destroys and where thieves do not break in and steal. For where your treasure is, there your heart will be also. The lamp of the body is the eye.
If therefore your eye is good, your whole body will be full of light. But if your eye is bad, your whole body will be full of darkness. If therefore the light that is in you is darkness, how great is that darkness?

Therefore I say to you, do not worry about your life, what you will eat or what you will drink; nor about your body, what you will put on.
Is not life more than food, and the body more than clothing? Look at the birds of the air, for they neither sow nor reap nor gather into barns; yet your Heavenly Father feeds them.
Are you not of more value than they? Which of you by worrying can add one cubit to his stature?
But seek first the kingdom of God and His righteousness, and all these things shall be added to you.
Therefore do not worry about tomorrow, for tomorrow will worry about its own things.
Sufficient for the day is its own trouble' (Matth 6:19-34)."

Valerian:
"Is that a mirror of myself being? This meets my notion of what it means to be cognizant of you, it means that I have to accept myself as I am."

God:
"Rest assured that I do love you, that I do love mankind. Life in its totality flows always in dependence of 'Deo concurrente'. I Am the light and the bearer of all aeons.[12]
You are sheltered and safe within me."

Valerian:
"How can you discern me from other living beings? Why do you talk to me?"

God:
"You called out to me."

Valerian:
"Yes, I did call you. I confessed that I wanted to live according to your will. You gave me an answer. Therefore I am important to you."

God:
"You were in a great spiritual predicament. There might come a time in your life, when you think that you are not important to me any longer, considering the millions of people on this

---

[12] Extract from 'Men, Fable, Myths'; Herbert Huber.

world. Trust me: not one of them will I forget.
Even the hairs on your head are counted. So do not be afraid. Just put your trust in me. And now my friend, we will end our conversation."
Valerian stammered and was quite agitated.
"Well but did you not, did you not say that you will be with me always."
God:
"I Am omnipresent."
Valerian:
"Your spirit is with me!"
God:
"And now you must go on and tell the people of our talk. Remember what you heard and keep it in your mind. I will be with you again but you will not know the hour. If you have learned to hear, you will hear what My Spirit will tell you."
Valerian:
"When you are standing before my door and when I hear your voice, I will open the door, you will come in and you will share my meal with me."
God:
"My Spirit is effused over all mankind. I will send signs on Heaven and Earth and everyone who calls My Name will be saved."
Valerian:
"How will that come to pass, will I really see you then?"
God:
"Ultimately, my Will decides."

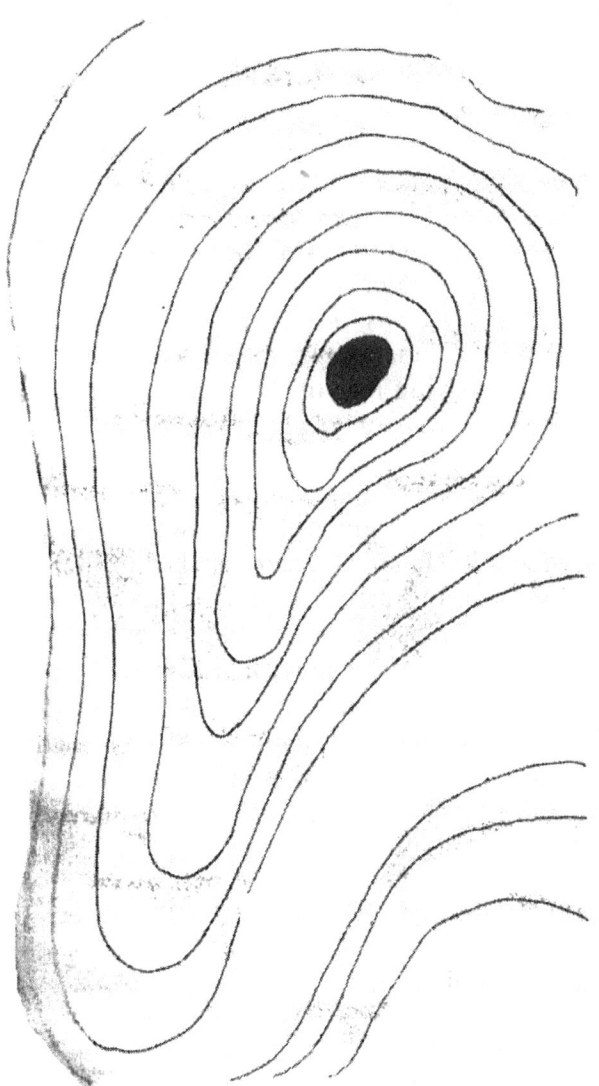

CHAPTER X

To be without a Soul

Do not despair When precious things are lost, Friends, joy and happiness. All will return in utter splendour.
What has to go must leave, What is our due remains with us.
For everything follows the laws That are high above ours,
Above our insight, and we fight them In seeming contradicttion. You have to live with yourself, And consider your entire life, The millions of possibilities, Of vast lands and emotions, Who know nothing of the past and Your losses.
Rainer Maria Rilke Valerian sat on the great terrace formed of rocks before the decaying ruin of the ancient temple, leaning his back against the wall of the fountain. He cherished this place.
It was here where he had met the snake.
He had watched him as he grabbed the flower of life with his jaws and devoured it. He himself had searched for the plant of wonders and wanted to snatch it from the snake, he stretched out his hands to grab it, but the snake slipped out of its old skin and escaped. This was the one change in his life. 'There is no doubt, that the snake exists', Valerian said. 'Does he know who he is? Is he something else that this body? How would he live if in the passage of time, in the passage of evolution he would have grown legs or wings, or fins, according to the necessary adaptation to the environment.
What would happen if the snake would not have to creep, but could walk like the lizards. But then it would not be a snake any more, what then? Then 'the Will of God' would not be valid any more. For did he not order: '*On your belly thou shall creep*' (1.Mos.3:14).
Now through all the millennia he crawled on the ground.
Did the snake ever want to live in another way, to be different? Valerian felt that the change that had happened to him had not touched his outer shell, but his self, his soul, his being, so that

he had become altered and reborn. He understood, that as he had passed through sleep and been changed, he would pass through death and be changed, and although remain himself in a new form of being. He did not fear death any more since he had the premonition that then we would be reunited with the God who had spoken to him. He felt his hand lying motionless on his legs.

The river, beneath the hill on which the temple stood, flowed unchanged and calm towards its destination. Far away at the turn of the river stood the ruins of another temple, the one the fire had destroyed when everything began. Valerian looked out with his eyes on the vast land before him. He searched for unknown sites and drank in the wonder of the moment. Calmness was within him.

Even his breath seemed to halt. No shadow of death. Sun, moon and stars ran their course. This was the present, the overwhelming scenery, clear and bright in the pure air. In this moment of light he felt invigorated, free from his former indolence, brought into a glittering reality.

Suddenly everything around him seemed simple and understandable.

No explanation was required, no thoughts, no words.

There were no questions, no necessity beyond the present experience. He felt only peace and quiet joy and that a great burden had been lifted from him. His breathing was free and easy. 'Have I found the secret of life?' he asked himself. 'But what use is this question? My error was to believe that I exist. As long as this error remained, I was a seeker. I had wishes. Their fulfilment did not quench the desire. Basically all this is quite simple.' He saw the immense sky above him and the snow covered mountain peaks in the distance. Nothing disturbed in between.

There was only a vast clearness. Is this a vision? How can something be so far away, when there is nothing it could be away from? Time had no place here. Valerian sat in silence and saw that there were uncountable signs of reasonable action of humans who populated the planet.

Small bridges spanned the rivers and lakes who reflected the stars. The hemisphere turned away from the sun was covered with myriads of mysterious lights. Tired of his loneliness he asked himself how it would be, if he could make a human being according to his wishes. How long would it take until he would develop a language, so that a mutual understanding would be possible. A beetle he had never seen before crawled on his foot. On the leaves of a broad bush he saw small ants and insects.

What were they doing here? He saw in astonishment the multitude of birds hiding in the tree above him. All these forms of life have their own importance, make their contribution to life, they are here and all have a special purpose. Why does this world not have quite different properties? 'There is no doubt that specific objects do exist and the world consists of all of them. I could just ask how they interact, how they exist and in what form and so on... The fact of their existence is indisputable.

With this decision God could prove his own existence. Did he do it? He gave me the opportunity to believe in His existence. He did not force me to believe unconditionally.'

The more he contemplated and looked about him into the distant landscape the more he saw the divine influence all around him and decided that he would have to walk backwards to decipher these wonders. 'How far would I have to go,' he spoke without a voice and without a question.

He remembered that someone had told him: There is a place where there is neither earth, nor water nor fire or air. It is not the place of the infinity of space or the infinity of consciousness, nor the spot of non existence, neither the sphere where there is no imagination or nonimagination.

It is not this world or another one, be it the moon or the sun. I call it neither the coming nor the going, neither standstill nor passing or beginning. It is without support, without a beginning, without a foundation, it is only the ending of suffering.

'Where there is dependence on each other there is movement, where there is no interdependence there is no movement.

Where there is no movement there is calm. Where there is calmness there is not desire. Where there is no desire there is no coming and going. Where there is no coming and going there is no death and rebirth. Where there is no death and rebirth there is no real world nor a netherworld, nor anything in between, it is the end of suffering.' Valerian looked up at the starlit sky, he fought his wish to call to God in this hour and ask him about the sense of human suffering, but this desire died down and his inner calm prevailed.

Suddenly he heard the rustling of leaves in the bushes near the fountain. He was quite terrified when the shadow of a man appeared like fog out of the twilight. Fear overtook Valerian and motionless he stared frightfully at the stranger.

A voice called to him out of the shadow, the dark one sat inclined against the tree trunk. The shadow whispered: "I am the man who believes that spirit and matter exist independently from each other. I am sure that they are two different manifestations. You should know, that I am very ill, that I suffer horrible pain, and all I desire is death. I do not contemplate suicide. I fear that other humans would suffer by my death and besides I consider suicide because of ethical reasons despicable.

Lastly I cannot exclude that there might be a life after death. I would not want to risk eternal damnation.

Therefore I am quite desperate."

Valerian was surprised and looked at him quite astonished.

"What can I alter here? What can I do for you?" He clearly remembered the admonishment of God how important it was that mortals should help each other.

"Why did you seek me out?" he asked the stranger. "I do not ask you from where you did come, or how you would know that I am here."

The stranger: "I know all this. Oh, yes, I have been observing you for quite a long time.

I have a question for you. Listen and give me your attention. A wondrous potion has been developed. Its marvellous effect is that the soul of the person who swallows it will be completely dissolved. This will happen in a way that the bodily functions will not be affected at all. The potion leaves no detectable traces of a change.

The body will continue to act as if he still possessed a soul. Even good friends and judicious observers could not detect until now if someone had taken the drug, if the person would not admit it himself.

Do you consider such a drug principally impossible? If you thought such a potion existed, would you take it yourself?"

Valerian:

"I would consider that immoral. Would it not mean the same as suicide?"

The stranger:

"It is certain that the body will fulfil all requirements further, the body will be alive and not dead. In this context I tell you: I take this drug and inform you about the fact. Thus you would know that I do not have a soul any more. In my behaviour there will be no difference.

What will your feelings tell you about this?"

Valerian:

"I don't know."

The stranger:

"This means that I can dissolve my soul. Tomorrow I will visit the scientist to acquire the drug from him. Then the period of my suffering will be over."

With these words he left. Excited and astonished Valerian did not stay long. He decided without deliberation to help the stranger in his unhappy situation, as well as he could.

He sought out the scientist and acquired the drug.

In the night he sneaked up to the house of the stranger and watched him. When the man fell into a deep sleep he crept into the house, to the bed and administered the drug. Then he sat down in the shadow of the house and waited.

The next morning the body of the stranger, now without a soul, awoke. He got out of bed and went straight to the scientist to get the drug and he bought it as well.

Then he returned to his house and spoke to himself: "Now all my suffering will come to an end." He took the drug and waited for a while until it would work. When the required time was over he called out angrily: "Damnation that stuff did not work at all. Clearly I do still have my soul and I am suffering just as before."[13]

Valerian was convinced that something here was quite wrong.

Evidently it was impossible that the sufferer could annihilate his soul to free himself from his affliction. The soul could not be dissolved by a drug and leave a soulless being without any feeling behind.

Valerian was sure of the temptation. He had doubted that the soul is the core, expressing how and what one is. He knew that letting go without the will of God was impossible.

Valerian felt himself too insignificant to unravel the wonders of life. Then out of nowhere he heard a voice:

"Valerian, imagine a universe completely free of souls, an utterly mechanical universe without the least trace of free will, conscience and without an observer anywhere.

This universe might be subject to a strict determinism or be filled with random, accidental, incalculable and groundless incidents. It would be however be determined by rules so that stable structures could form and develop. In such a universe a hub of quite different solidly constructed selfsufficient objects would exist, each of them having an inner representative system, complex enough to form a full and detail rich self image. With each of these objects this would evoke the illusion of freedom of will, where in reality it would be a soulless universe and the objects populating it would be nothing than machines tied to rules, moving in a predetermined way und pretending to exchange meaningful ideas.

In reality the image and sending of prolonged sequences of void, hollow waves would lead to a mechanical prattle and chatter. Could you imagine such a strange universe?

---

[13] Extracts from Raymond M. Smullyan 'the unfortunate Dualist'; in 'The Book Needs No Title.'

Now you can get a glimpse in this universe and see all of mankind in its disoriented light." And He foretold him: *"The life, that you seek you will not find on earth."*
Valerian felt sure of his self-awareness and felt thankful to know there was a difference to those empty bundles of reflexes.

Why do you need
To prove there is a God?
Would you light a torch
In order to see the sun?

(Wisdom of the East)

And then he was gone

God had taken him away.
We have to assume that in our time Valerian can not be taken as an example neither for men nor for women. The Bible is very precise about a person's ancestors. People then wanted to know where you came from and where we were going to.
'No man is an island', in the context of the Bible this is quite obvious and there is no need to dwell on this further. We can see that for Valerian the world was totally new when he entered it. So many things he had to explore, how to catch fish, how to prepare food, how to make tools and what attitude to take with humans and animals.
He never built a house, nor a shed to shield him from the sun.
When he came into life he just lived and he lived in community with God.
Suddenly he ceased to be for God had taken him away.
Maybe we could call him a 'driving force' or somebody who knew exactly what he desired, he wanted to live without a sin. He lived in community with God, in other words a long life. There is not more to know. No funeral, no memorial speeches, no monument carved from stone.
God did take him away.
He just vanished like the frosty fog on the fields dissolving in the warmth of the sun on a spring morning.

What an incredible provocation for us humans, who are convinced that every human will leave a trace. Did Valerian do any work? We do not know. Maybe he did not work at all. Did he make a career, he did not. Did he complete something great, not at all. Maybe he went hunting, like Nimrod the renowned huntsman. Nothing has been mentioned about him. No word about his prowess in the field of war. He never vanquished anyone and never conquered a fortress. Evidently nothing important ever happened to him. What about women?

Did he have children? Did he build something, at least a wall or a well? Valerian did not build anything.

He did not build a shed, no well, no ark, no tower of Babylon, no wall around a town, not even an altar, and that is really strange.

A provoking absence of all the things which make humans man and that could be mentioned in the scriptures of the ancient fathers.

There is no material imprint of his life. Just the unbelievable, faded trace in a script: 'Valerian lived in community with God'.

Should that be something? Such a person will never pay taxes. A wife or any woman would only have problems with such a kind of man. What should she answer to the question: "What does your husband do?"

Valerian disappeared in the middle of the story, without a trace in history.

Do not look for a burial mound or the signs of memory. One beautiful day he cut the thin veil that separates the visible from the invisible world and stepped directly into the light. Some brief words from Valerian give the heart of the matter: The life of a man can be complete even when he created nothing of a lasting duration. He may be worth remembering although he did not even build a shed, because all his life was dedicated to God. We may presume that God looked favourably on the life of Valerian.

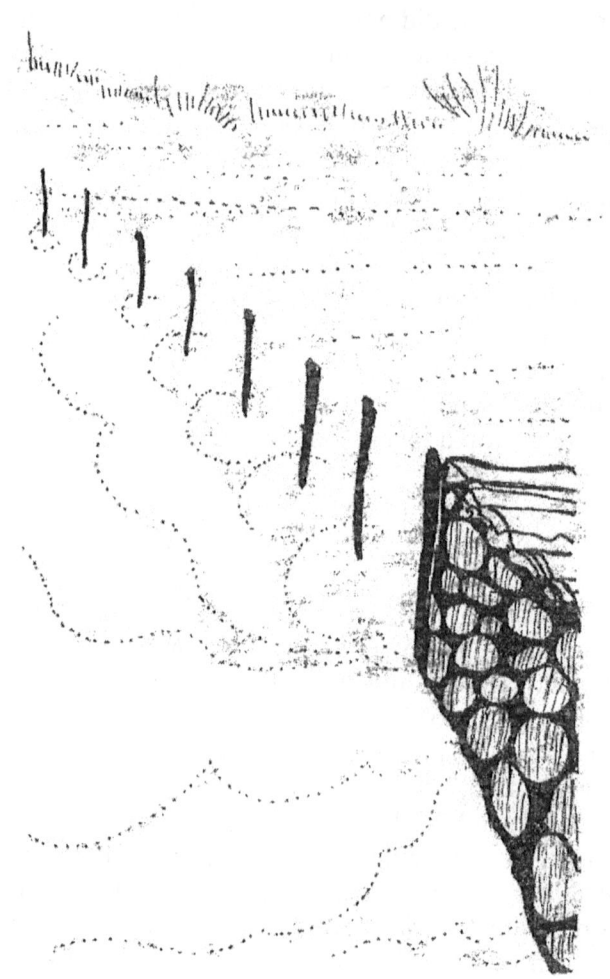

Valerian gains wisdom

‚What will you do in this world?'
asked Seng Ts'an the great Zen-poet.
Valerian gave his answer thus:
'The world has already been made.
The Lord of Creation considered it all, my lot has been cast, my journey is done.
What Salomon taught me gave me wisdom.
My presumption to be able to live without a free will, was just as wrong as the desire of the stranger to be without a soul and therefore without pain.
It is not easy to recognize the will of God, it is even more difficult to accept it and to obey.
And Valerian called out into the uncertainty:
"Listen, you unknown stranger, wherever you are and whoever you might be:

1. Remember the vainness of all earthly matter

1 This is as it has always been and will remain so forever."
2 »Vanity of vanities,« says the Preacher; vanity of Vanities, all is vanity.«
3 What profit has a man from all his labour in which he toils under the sun?
4 *One* generation passes away,
and *another* generation comes; but the Earth abides forever.....
5 The sun also rises, and the sun
goes down, and hastens to the place where it arose.
6 The wind goes toward the south, and turns around to the north; The wind whirls about continually, and comes again on its circuit.
7 All the rivers run into the sea, yet the sea is not full; to the place from which the rivers come, there they return again.
8 All things are full of labour, man cannot express it.
The eye is not satisfied with seeing, nor the ear filled with hearing.

9 That which has been is what will be, that which is done is what will be done, and *there is* nothing new under the sun.
10 Is there anything of which it may be said, »See, this is new?« It has already been in ancient times before us.
11 *There* is no remembrance of former things, nor will there be any remembrance of *things* that are to come by *those* who will come after.
12 I, the Preacher, was king over Israel in Jerusalem.
13 And I set my heart to seek and search out by wisdom concerning all that is done under heaven; this burdensome task God has given to the sons of man, by which they may be exercised.
14 I have seen all the works that are done under the sun; and indeed, all is vanity and grasping for the wind.
15 What is crooked cannot be made straight, and what is lacking cannot be numbered.
16 I command with my heart, saying "Look, I have attained greatness, and have gained more wisdom than all who were before me in Jerusalem.
My heart has understood great wisdom and knowledge."
17 And I set my heart to know wisdom and to know madness and folly. I perceived that this also is grasping for the wind.
18 For in much wisdom is much grief, and he who increases knowledge increases sorrow.

2. The Vanity of Pleasure

1 And I said to my heart, "Come now, I will test you with mirth; therefore enjoy pleasure"; but surely, this also was vanity.
2 I said of laughter – "Madness!"; and of mirth, "What does it accomplish?"
3 I searched in my heart how to gratify my flesh with wine, while guiding my heart with wisdom, and how to lay hold on folly, till I might see what was good for the sons of men to do under heaven all the days of their lives.
4 I made my works great. I built myself houses, and planted myself vineyards.

5 I made myself gardens and orchards, and I planted all *kinds* of fruit trees in them.
6 I made myself water pools from which to water the growing trees of the grove.
7 I acquired male and female servants, and had servants born in my house. Yes, I had greater possessions of herds and flocks than all who were in Jerusalem before me.
8 I also gathered for myself silver and gold and the special treasures of kings and of the provinces.
I acquired male and female singers, the delights of the sons of men, and musical instruments of all kinds.
9 So I became great and excelled more than all who were before me in Jerusalem. Also my wisdom remained with me.
10 Whatever my eyes desired, I did not keep from them.
I did not withhold my heart from any pleasure.
For my heart rejoiced in all my labour; and this was my reward from all my labour.
11 Then I looked on all the works that my hands had done
And on the labour in which I had toiled; and indeed, all was vanity and grasping for the wind.
There was no profit under the sun.
12 Then I turned myself to consider wisdom and madness and folly; for what can the man do who succeeds the king? -
Only what he has already done
13 Then I saw that wisdom excels folly as light excels darkness.
14 The wise man's eyes are in his head, but the fool walks in darkness.
Yet I myself perceived That the same event happens to them all.
15 So I said in my heart, "As it happens to the fool, It also happens to me, and why was I then more wise?"
Then I said in my heart, "This also is vanity."
16 Fore *there is* no more remembrance of the wise than of the fool forever.
Since all that now is will be forgotten in the days to come.
And how does a wise *man* die?
As the fool.

17 Therefore I hated life because the work that was done under the sun was distressing to me, for all is vanity and grasping for the wind.
18 Then I hated all my labour in which I had toiled under the sun, because I must leave it to the man who will come after me.
19 And who knows whether he will be wise or a fool? Yet he will rule over all my labour in which I toiled and in which I have shown myself wise under the sun.
This also is vanity.
20 Therefore I turned my heart and despaired of all the labour in which I had toiled under the sun.
21 For there is a man, whose labour is with wisdom, knowledge, and skill; yet he must leave his heritage to a man who has not laboured for it. This also is vanity and a great evil.
22 For what has man for all his labour, and for the striving of his heart with which he has toiled under the sun?
23 For all his days are sorrowful, and his work burdensome; even in the night his heart takes no rest. This also in vanity.
24 Nothing is better for a man, than that he should eat and drink, and that his soul should enjoy good in his labour. This also, I saw, was from the hand of God.
25 For who can eat, or who can have enjoyment, more than I?
26 For God gives *wisdom* and knowledge and joy to a man who is good in His sight; but to the sinner.
He gives the work of gathering and collecting, that he may give to him who is good before God. This also is vanity and grasping for the wind. Everything a Season

3. To everything there is a season.

1 A time for every purpose under heaven.
2 A time to be born, and a time to die; a time to plant, and a tine to pluck what is planted;
3 A time to kill, and a time to heal; a time to break down, and a time to build up;

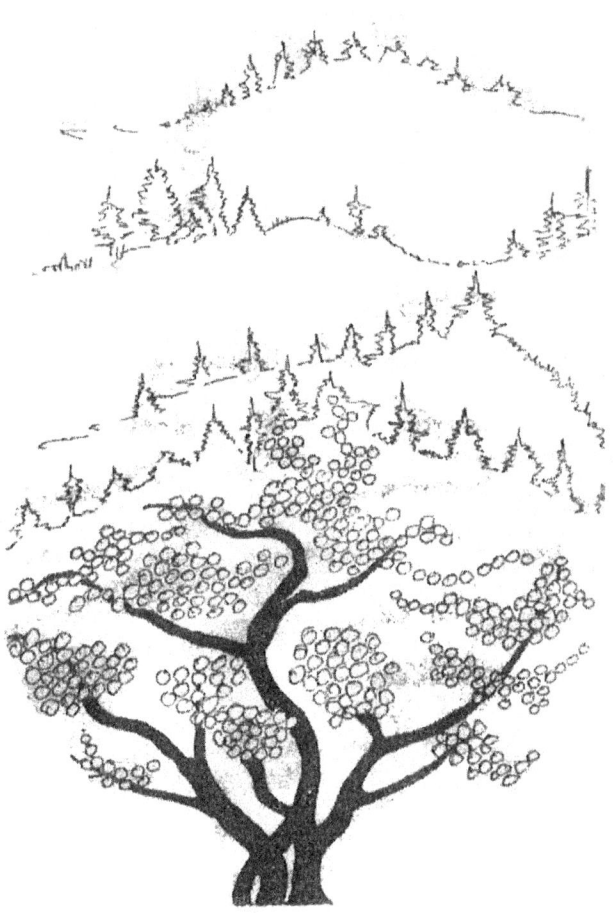

4 A time to weep, and a time to laugh; a time to mourn, and a time to dance.

5 A time to cast away stones, and a time to gather stones; a time to embrace, and a time to refrain from embracing;

6 A time to gain, and a time to lose; a time to keep, and a time to throw away;

7 A time to tear, and a time to sew; a time to keep silence, and a time to speak;

8 A time to love, and a time to hate; a time of war, and a time of peace.

10 I have seen a God-given task with which the son of men are to be occupied.

11 He has made everything beautiful in its time. Also he has put eternity in their hearts, except that no one can find out the work that God does from beginning to end.

12 I know that nothing is better for them than to rejoice, and to do good in their lives;

13 and also that every man should eat and drink and enjoy the good of all his labour – it is the gift of God.

14 I know that whatever God does, it shall be forever.
Nothing can be added to it, and nothing taken from it.
God does it, that men should fear before Him.

15 That which is has already been, and what is to be has already been; and God requires an account of what is past.

16 Moreover I saw under the sun: In the place of judgment, wickedness was there; and in the place of righteousness, iniquity was there.

17 I said in my heart, "God shall judge the righteous and the wicked, for there is a time there for every purpose and for every work."

18 I said in my heart: "Concerning the condition of the sons of men, God tests them, that they may see that they themselves are like animals."

19 For what happens to the sons of men also happens to animals, one thing befalls them: as one dies, so dies the other. Surely, they all have one breath: man has no advantage over animals, for all is vanity.

20 All go to one place: all are from the dust, and all return to the dust.

21 Who knows the spirit of the sons of men, which goes upward, and the spirit of the animal which goes down to the Earth?

22 So, I perceived that nothing *is* better than that a man should rejoice in his own works, for that *is* his heritage. For who can bring him to see what will happen after him?

4. The Vanity of Selfish Toil

1 Then I returned and considered all the oppression that is done under the sun: And look! The tears of the oppressed, but they have no comforter – On the side of their oppressions *there* is power, but they have no comforter.

2 Therefore I praised the dead who were already dead, more than the living who are still alive.

3 Yet, better than both is he who has never existed, who has not seen the evil work that is done under the sun.

4 Again, I saw that for all toil and every skilful work a man is envied by his neighbour. This also is vanity and grasping for the wind.

5 The fool folds his hands And consumes his own flesh.

6 Better a handful with quietness than both hands full, *together* with toil and grasping for the wind.

7 Then I returned, and saw vanity under the sun:

8 There is one alone, without companion:

Yet there is no end to all his labours, nor is his eye satisfied with riches.

But he never asks, "for whom do I toil and deprive myself of good?"

This also is vanity and a grave misfortune.

9 Two are better than one, because they have a good reward for their labour.

10 For if they fall, one will lift up his companion.

But woe to him who is alone when he falls?

For he has no one to help him up.

11 Again, if two lie down together, they will keep warm, but how can one warm alone?
12 Though one may be overpowered by another, two can withstand him.
And a threefold cord is not quickly broken.
13 Better a poor and wise youth than a old and foolish king who will be admonished no more.
14 For he comes out of prison to be king, although he was born poor in his kingdom.
15 I saw all the living who walk under sun;
They were with the second youth who stands in his place.
16 There was no end of all the people over whom he was made king; yet those who come afterward will not rejoice in him.
Surely this also is vanity and grasping for the wind.

5. The vanity of Gain

1 Walk prudently when you go to the house of God; and draw ear to hear rather than to give the sacrifice of fools, for they do not know that they do evil.
2 Do not be rash with your mouth, and let not your heart utter anything hastily before God.
For God is in heaven, and you on earth.
Therefore let your words be few.
3 For a dream comes through much activity, and a fool's voice is known by his many words.
4 When you make a vow to God, do not delay to pay it; for He has no pleasure in fools.
Pay what you have vowed –
5 Better not to vow than to vow and not pay.
6 Do not let your mouth cause your flesh to sin, nor say before he messenger *of* God that it *was* an error.
Why should God be angry at our excuse and destroy the work for your hands?

7 For in the multitude of dreams and many words *there* is also vanity. But fear God.

8 If you see the oppression of the poor, and the violent perversion of justice and righteousness in a province, do not marvel at the matter, for high official watches over high official, and higher officials are over them.
9 Moreover the profit of the land is for all; even the king is served from the field:
10 He, who loves silver will not be satisfied with silver; nor he who loves abundance, with increase this also is vanity.
11 When goods increase, they increase who eat them; so what profit have the owners except to see them with their eyes?
12 The sleep of a labouring man is sweet, whether he eats little or much; but the abundance of the rich will not permit to sleep.
13 There is a severe evil which I have seen under the sun:
Riches kept for their owner to his hurt.
14 But those riches perish through misfortune; when he begets a son, there is nothing in his hand.
15 As he came from the mother's womb, naked shall he return, To go as he came.
And he shall take nothing from his labour which he may carry in his hand.
16 And this also is a severe evil – Just exactly as he came, so shall he go.
And what profit has he who has laboured for the wind?
17 All his days he also eats in darkness, and he has much sorrow and sickness and anger.
18 Here is, what I have seen: *It is* good an fitting *for one* to eat and drink, and to enjoy the good of all his labour in which he toils under the sun all the days of his *life* which God gives him: for it *is* his heritage.
19 As for every man to whom God has given riches and wealth, and given him power to eat of it, to receive his heritage and rejoice in his labour – *this is* the *gift* of God.
20 For he will not dwell unduly on the days of his life, because God keeps *him* busy, the joy of his heart.

6. There is an evil which I have seen under the sun,

1 And it *is* common among men:
2 A man, to whom God has given riches and wealth and honour, so that he lacks nothing for himself of all he desires; yet God does not give him power to eat of it, but a foreigner consumes it. This is vanity, and it is an evil affliction.
3 If a man begets a hundred children and lives many years, so that the days of his years are many; but his soul is not satisfied with goodness, or indeed he has no burial, I say, *that* a stillborn child is better than he - 4 for it comes in vanity and departs in darkness, and its name is covered with darkness. 5 Though it
has not seen the sun or known *anything*, this has more rest than that man, 6 even if he lives a thousand years twice – but has not seen goodness.
Do not all go to one place?
7 All the labour of man is for his mouth, and yet the soul is not satisfied.
8 For what more has the wise *man* than the fool?
What does the poor man have, who knows *how* to walk before the living?
9 Better is the sight of the eyes than the wandering of desire.
This also is vanity and grasping for the wind.
10 Whatever one is, he has been named already, for it is knows that he is man; and he cannot contend with Him who is mightier than he.
11 Since there are many things that increase vanity, how is man the *better*?
12 For who knows what is *good* for man in life, all the days of his vain life which he passes like a shadow?
Who can tell a man what will happen after him under the sun?

7. A Good Name is Better

1 A good name is better than precious ointment, and the day of death than the day of one's birth;
2 Better to go to the house of mourning than to go to the house of feasting, for that is the end of all men; and the living will take it to heart.
3 Sorrow is better than laughter, for by a sad countenance the heart is made better.
4 The heart of the wise is in the house of mourning, but the heart of fool is in the house of mirth.
5 It is better to hear the rebuke of the wise than for a man to hear the song of fools.
6 For like the crackling of thorns under a pot, so is the laughter of the fool.
This is also vanity.
7 Surely oppression destroys a wise *man's* reason, and a bribe debases the heart.
8 The end of a thing is better than its beginning, the patient in spirit is better than the proud in spirit.
9 Do not hasten in your spirit to be angry, for anger rests in the bosom of fools.
10 Do not say: "Why were the former days better than these?" For you do not inquire wisely concerning this.
11 Wisdom is good with an inheritance, and profitable to those who see the sun.
12 For wisdom is a defence as money is a defence, but the excellence of knowledge is that wisdom gives life to those who have it.
13 Consider the work of God; for who can make straight what He has made crooked?
14 In the day of prosperity be joyful, but in the day of adversity consider: Surely God has appointed the one as well as the other. So that man can find out nothing that *will* come after him.
15 I have seen everything in my days of vanity: There is a just *man* who perishes in his righteousness, and there is a wicked *man* who prolongs *life* in his wickedness.

16 Do not be overly righteous, nor be overly wise: Why should you destroy yourself?

17 Do not be overly wicked, nor be foolish: Why should you die before your time?

18 It is good that you grasp this, and also not remove your hand from the other; for he who fears God will escape them all.

19 Wisdom strengthens the wise more than ten rulers of the city.

20 For there is not a just man on earth who does good and does not sin.

21 Also do not take to heart everything people say.
Lest you hear your servant cursing you.

22 For many times, also, your own heart has known, that even you have cursed others.

23 All this I have proved by wisdom.
I said: "I will be wise"; but it was far from me.

24 As for that which is far off and exceedingly deep. Who can find it out?

25 I applied my heart to know, to search and seek out wisdom and the reason of things, to know the wickedness of folly,
Even of foolishness and madness.

26 And I find more bitter than death the woman whose heart is snares and nets, whose hands *are* fetters.
He who pleases God shall escape from her, but the sinner shall be trapped by her.

27 "Here is what I have found," says the Preacher, "*Adding* one thing to the other, to find out the reason,

28 Which my soul still seeks but I cannot find: One man among a thousand I have found, but a woman among all these
I have not found.

29 Truly, this only I have found: That God made man upright, but they have sought out many schemes."

8. Death comes to all

1 Who is like a wise man? And who knows the interpretation of a thing?
A man's wisdom makes his face shine, and the sternness of his face is changed.
2 I *say*, "Keep the king's commandment for the sake of your oath to God.
3 Do not be hasty to go from his presence. Do not take your stand for an evil thing, for he does whatever pleases *him*."
4 Where the word of a King is, *there* is power; and who many say to him: "What are you doing?"
5 He who keeps his command will experience nothing harmful; and a wise man's heart discerns both time und judgment,
6 Because for every matter there is a time and judgment. Though the misery of man increases greatly.
7 For he does not know what will happen; so who can tell him when it will occur?
8 No one has power over the spirit to retain the spirit, and no one has power in the day of death.
There is no release from that war, and wickedness will not deliver those who are given to it.
9 All this I have seen, and applied my heart to every work that is done under the sun: *There* is a time in which one man rules over another to his own hurt.
10 Then I saw the wicked buried, who had come and gone from the place of holiness, and they were forgotten in the city where they had so done. This also *is vanity*.
11 Because the sentence against an evil work is not executed speedily, therefore the heart of the sons of men is fully set in them to do evil.
12 Though a sinner does evil a hundred *times*, and his *days* are prolonged, yet, I surely know that it will be well with those who fear God, who fear before Him.
13 But it will not be well with the wicked, nor will he prolong his days, *which* are as a shadow, because he does not fear before God.

14 There is a vanity which occurs on earth, that there are just *men* to whom it happens according to the work of the wicked; again, there are wicked *men* to whom it happens according to the work of the righteous, I said that this also is vanity.

15 So I commanded enjoyment, because a man has nothing better under the sun than to eat, drink, and be merry; for this will remain with him in his labour *all* the days of his life which God gives him under the sun.

16 When I applied my heart to know wisdom and to see the business that is done on earth, even though one sees no sleep day or night.

17 Then I saw all the work of God, that a man cannot find out he work that is done under the sun. For though a man labours to discover it, yet he will not find it; moreover, though a wise *man* attempts to know it, he will not be able to find it.

9. The race not to the swift

1 For I considered all this in my heart, so that I could declare it all: that the righteous and the wise and their works are in the hand of God. People know neither love nor hatred by anything *they see* before them.

2 All things *come* alike to all: *One event happens to the righteous and the wicked; to the good, the clean, and the unclean; to him who sacrifices and him, who does not sacrifice.*
As is the good, so is the sinner. He who takes an oath as he
who fears an oath.

3 This is an evil in all that is done under the sun: that one thing *happens* to all. Truly the hearts of the sons of men are full of the evil; madness is in their hearts while they live, and after that *they* go to the dead.

4 But for him, who is joined to all the living there is hope, for a living dog is better than a dead lion.

5 For the living know that they will die; But the dead know nothing.
And they have no more reward, for the memory of them is forgotten.

6 Also their love, their hatred, and their envy have now perished. Nevermore will they have a share In anything done under the sun.

7 Go, eat your bread with joy, and drink your wine with a merry heart; for God has already accepted your works.

8 Let your garments always be white, and let your head lack no oil.

9 Live joyfully with the wife whom you love all the days of your vain life which He has given you under the sun, all your days of vanity; for that is your portion in life, and in the labour which you perform under the sun.

10 Whatever your hand finds to do, do it with your might, for there is no work or device or knowledge or wisdom in the grave where you are going.

11 I returned and saw under the sun that – *The race is not to the swift, nor the battle to the strong, nor bread to the wise, nor*

riches to men of understanding, nor favour to men of skill; but time and chance happen to them all.

12 For man also does not know his time: Like fish taken in a cruel net;   like birds caught in a snare;   so the sons of men are snared in an evil time; when it falls suddenly upon them.

13 This wisdom I have also seen under the sun, and it *seemed* great to me.

14 *There was* a little city with few men in it; and a great king came against it, besieged it, and built great snares around it.

15 Now there was found in it a poor wise man, and he by his wisdom delivered the city. Yet no one remembered that same poor man.

16 Then I said: "Wisdom is *better* than strength; nevertheless the poor man's wisdom is despised, and his words are not heard.

17 Words of the wise, *spoken* quietly, *should* be heard rather than the shout of a ruler of fools.

18 Wisdom is better than weapons of war; but one sinner destroys much good."

10. Fair dos for all

1 Dead flies putrefy the perfumer's ointment, and cause it to live off a foul odour; so does a little folly to one respected for wisdom and honour.
2 A wise man's heart is at his right hand, but a fool's heart is at his left.
3 Even when a fool walks along the way, he lacks wisdom, and he shows everyone that he is a fool.
4 If the spirit of the ruler rises against you, do not leave your post, for conciliation pacifies great offenses.
5 There is an evil I have seen under the sun.
As an error proceeding from the ruler:
6 Folly is set in great dignity, while the rich sit in a lowly place.
7 I have seen servants on horses, while princes walk on the ground like servants.
8 He, who digs a bit will fall into it, and whoever breaks through a wall will be bitten by a serpent.
9 He who quarries stones may be hurt by them; and he, who splits wood may be endangered by it.
10 If the ax is dull; and one does not sharpen the edge, then he must use more strength; but wisdom brings success.
11 A serpent may bite when it is not charmed; the babbler is no different.
12 The words of a wise man's mouth *are* gracious, but the lips of a fool shall swallow him up;
13 The words of his mouth begin with foolishness, and the end of his talk is raving madness.
14 A fool also multiplies words.
No man knows what is to be; who can tell him what will be after him?
15 The labour of fools wearies them, for they do not even know how to go to the city!
16 Woe to you. O Land, when your king *is* a child, and your princes feast in the morning!

17 Blessed *are* you, O land, when your king is the son of nobles, and your princes feast at the proper time – for strength and not for drunkenness!

18 Because of laziness the building decays, and through idleness of hands the house leaks.

19 A feast is made for laughter, and wine makes merry; but money answers everything.

20 Do not curse the king, even in your thought. Do not curse the rich, even in your bedroom; for a bird of the air may carry your voice, and a bird in flight may tell the matter.

11. Cast your bread

1 Cast your bread upon the waters, for you will find it after many days.

2 Give a serving to seven, and also to eight, for you do not know what evil will be on the earth.

3 If the clouds are full of rain, they empty themselves upon the earth; and if the tree falls to the south or the north, in the place where the tree falls, there it shall lie.

4 He, who observes the wind will not sow, and he who regards the clouds will not reap.

5 As you do not know what is the way of the wind, or how the bones grow in the womb of her who is with child, so you do not know the works of God who makes everything.

6 In the morning sow your seed, and in the evening do not withhold your hand; for you do not know which will prosper, either this or that, or whether both alike will be good.

7 Truly the light is sweet, and it is pleasant for the eyes to behold the sun; 8 But if a man lives many years and rejoices in them all, yet let him remember the days of darkness, for they will be many.

All that is coming *is* vanity.

9 Rejoice, O, young man, in your youth, and let your heart cheer you in the days of your youth; walk in the ways of your heart, and in the sight of your eyes; but know that for all these God will bring you into judgment.

10 Therefore remove sorrow from your heart, and put away evil from your flesh, for childhood and youth *are vanity.*

12 Remember your creator.

1. Remember now your Creator in the days of your youth, before the difficult days come, and the years draw near when you say, *"I have no pleasure in them"*:
2 While the sun and the light the moon and the stars, are not darkened, and the clouds do not return after the rain;
3 In the day, when the keepers of the house tremble, and the strong men bow down. When the grinders cease because they are few, and those that look through the windows grow dim.
4 When the doors are shut in the streets, and the sound of grinding is low. When one rises up at the sound of a bird, and all the daughters of music are brought low.
5 Also they are afraid of height, and of terrors in the way. When the almond tree blossoms, the grasshopper is a burden. And desire fails, for man goes to his eternal home, and the mourners go about the streets.
6 *Remember your Creator* before the silver cord is loosed, or the golden bowl is broken, or the pitcher shattered at the fountain, or the wheel broken in the well.
7 Then the dust will return to the earth as it was, and the spirit will return to God who gave it.
8 *"Vanity of vanities,"* says the *Preacher.*
"All is vanity."
9 And *moreover*, because the Preacher was wise, he still taught the people knowledge; yes, he pondered and sought out and set in order many proverbs.
10 The Preacher sought to find acceptable words; and *what was* written was upright – words of truth.
11 The words of the wise are like goads, and the words of scholars are like well-driven nails, given by one Shepherd.
12 And further, my son, be admonished by these. Of making many books *there* is no end, and much study is wearisome to the flesh.

13 *Let us hear the conclusion of the whole matter: Fear God and keep His commandments, for this is man's all.*
14 *For God will bring every work into judgment, including every secret thing, whether good or evil.*

Ecclesiastes:[14]

---

[14] Ecclesiastes:
Written by King Salomon, about 940 B.C., Ecclesiastes shares the mature wisdom of one who, near the end of his life, looks to realize that only a life lived for God is a life fulfilled.

Sources:

The New Possibility Thinkers Bible by Paul David Dunn, Dr. Robert H. Schuller, executive editor, New King James Version Thomas Nelson Publishers Nashville 1982.
Buber Martin, *Ich und Du' (I and You)* Publisher Lambert Schneider, Heidelberg ,1983
Goethe v. J. W. Verse, Trost bei Goethe', *(Consolation by Goethe)* Publisher W. Scheuermann, Wien, 1941
Huber, Herbert, Dr. ‚Menschen. Märchen, Mythen'; (Men, Fable, Myths) Publisher Mut , Asendorf 1990
Borges, Jorge Luis 'Labyrinthe' 1959 The Mind Publisher Basic Books, Inc. New York 1981 (free translation by oneself)
Bytschkow, Victor, Dr. 'Love is a foundation of Human existence'; Voice of the Orthodoxy, Moscow 1988
D.E. Harding, 'On having no Head' Perennial Library, Rediscovering the Mind Library, Harper & Row, 1972
Lem, Stanislaw, ‚Die vollkommene Leere', (The total Void) aus ‚Kyberiade'; Publisher Insel - Frankfurt 1982
Morowitz, Herold 'Psychology Today', Rediscovering the Mind, August 1980
Platon, - Staatschriften Prof. Dr. Othmar Spann, Die Herdflamme', (The flame of the Hearth' Bd. 6 – Essays on the State' 2.Part) zweiter Teil, Staat. Publisher - Gustav Fischer, Jena 1925
Richard Dawkins 'The Selfish Gene' Oxford University Press 1976
Raymond M. Smullyan 'The Tao is Silent' Harper & Row Publisher, New York 1977. 'An unfortunate Dualist'- 'The Book Needs No Title'. 1980 Prentice-Hall, Englewood Cliffs New York
Rotter, Hans, ‚Grundgebot Liebe', (Basic Command Love') Publisher Tyrolia , Innsbruck 1983 (Chap. Love and society)
Schopenhauer, Arthur, ‚Aphorismen zur Lebensweisheit' (aphorism and worldly wisdom) Publiher - Alfred Kröner, Leipzig
Wheelis, Allen 'On not Knowing How to live'. Harper & Row 1975

References Bracketed

1. 1. John. First Letters of St. John (New Testament)
2. 1. Cor. First Letter of the Apostle Paul to the Corinthians (New Testament)
3. 2. Cor. Second Letter of the Apostle Paul to the Corinthians (New Testament)
4. Gen. The Book Genesis; The first Book Moses (Old Testament)
5. John. Gospel of St. John (New Testament)
6. Rom. Letter of the Apostle Paul to the Romans (New Testament)
7. Luk. Gospel of the Apostle Luke (New Testament)
8. Math. Gospel of the Apostle Matthew (New Testament)
9. Ex. The second Book of Moses (Old Testament)
10. The Ecclesiastes. The Song of Salomon 940 B.C. (Old Testament)

The day will come
When God will take away
All tears from your eyes.
When death will be no more
Nor grief and sorrow
Nor pain because
Bygones will be
In the past.

St. John. Revelation 21.4

BIOGRAPHY

Katharina Beta, born in Berlin, has taken up residence 1984 in Vienna. Since then she works as a free lance writer.

Mrs. Beta has studied medicine and later the history of the Eastern Churches as well as philosophy. In 2004 she started her bible studies in California, USA.

Mrs. Beta is a member of the Catholic Foundation 'Pro Orien-te' and is highly interested in ecumenical work with the young generation.

She has published a series of books and was invited to several public lectures. Publications in German: ‚Ikonenverehrung der orthodoxen Ostkirche' (*Worship of Icons in the Eastern Orthodox churches*); Eine Flamme erfülle sein Herz - das Leben des Starez Siluan auf dem Berg Athos'; *('A heart enflamed – life of the Starets Siluan* on the Mount Athos'); ‚Die Russische Seele'; Christianisierung Russlands; ('Russian Soul'; the Christianization of Russia); 'Das Kiewer Höhlenkloster als Wiege russischen Mönchtums'; (The Kiev monastery of caves – the cradle of Russian monk culture; 'Malermönch Andrej Rubljow'; *(The great painter and monk Andrei Roubliev)*; A trilogy for young readers: 'Janus'; (‚*Ianus'*); ‚Wenn wir alle nackt wären'; (*'If we all were naked'*); ‚Das Einfache ist das Größte'; (*'The simple things are the important ones'*); Then she wrote the autobiography 'Katharsis' (Catharsis). This book was a bestseller.

Followed by 'Erkennst Du mich?' (*'Do you recognize me?'*) *Dialogue with Arthur Schopenhauer as a way to help you organize your life*; 'Bist Du der, auf den ich gewartet habe',

(Katharsis II); (‚*Are you the one I was waiting for?'* *(Catharsis II)*); ‚Ich liebe mich', (Roman); (*'I love myself', (a novel)*);

Mrs. Beta is highly interested in scientific research work on Madagascar, in the studies on the use of solar energy and the preservation of the rain forest. ‚Sei wie ein Baum', (Roman); (*'Be like a tree', (a novel)*).

In the United States she was highly impressed with the reformed Evangelical Church and especially with the positive way of thinking and living of Dr. Schuller. 'Ultimately – the Will of God decides.' Ultimately - letztendlich gilt Gottes Wille.'

'*Jesus was born for you* '(*When was Jesus actually born*?);

'Jesus ist für dich geboren' (Wann ist Jesus wirklich geboren?).

New books are to come soon.

www.ingramcontent.com/pod-product-compliance
Lightning Source LLC
Chambersburg PA
CBHW050632160426
43194CB00010B/1636